THE ULTIMATE COCKNEY GEEZER'S
GUIDE TO RHYMING SLANG

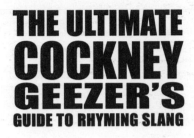

D0566653

THE ULTIMATE COCKNEY GEEZER'S

GUIDE TO RHYMING SLANG

Geoff Tibballs

EBURY
PRESS

3 5 7 9 10 8 6 4 2

Published in 2008 by Ebury Press, an imprint of Ebury Publishing

A Random House Group Company

Text © Geoff Tibballs 2008
Illustrations © Anthony Cockayne 2008

Geoff Tibballs has asserted his right to be identified
as the author of this Work in accordance with the
Copyright, Designs and Patents Act 1988

The Random House Group Limited Reg. No. 954009

Addresses for companies within the Random House Group
can be found at www.randomhouse.co.uk

A CIP catalogue record for this book
is available from the British Library

The Random House Group Limited supports The Forest
Stewardship Council (FSC), the leading international forest
certification organisation. All our titles that are printed on
Greenpeace approved FSC certified paper carry the FSC logo.
Our paper procurement policy can be found at
www.rbooks.co.uk/environment

Designed and set by seagulls.net

Printed in the UK by CPI Cox & Wyman, Reading, RG1 8EX

ISBN 9780091927486

To my bread knife
and two bottles of water

INTRODUCTION

If you ask most people outside London whether they regularly use Cockney rhyming slang, they would probably answer, 'Not on your Nellie!' – blissfully unaware that 'not on your Nellie' is itself a derivative of Cockney rhyming slang, from 'Nellie Duff' meaning 'puff', which is slang for 'life'. So 'not on your Nellie' means 'not on your life'. That's the thing about rhyming slang – we often don't realise that we're using it. So many of its words and phrases have entered mainstream language – 'titfer' (hat), 'use your loaf' (use your head), 'bread' (money) to name but three – that if you deny ever having spoken it you're either talking cobbler's (cobbler's awls = balls) or telling porkies (pork pies = lies).

So how did this curious language that both delights and baffles foreign tourists come about? The first mention of it is in John Camden Hotten's 1859 book *The Slang Dictionary* and the popularly held belief is that it was designed by criminals and shady street sellers as a secret code indecipherable to outsiders, especially the police. Over the next 100 years it was adopted by working-class Cockneys in general – often to provide euphemisms for embarrassing conditions or situations – and has recently enjoyed a new lease of life among teenagers who, not content with having their own street language, have been attracted by the humour, ingenuity, irreverence and air of mystery of Cockney rhyming slang. Consequently new phrases are continually being invented, often invoking modern celebrities such as Ricky Gervais, Johnny Depp or Ant and Dec. Having your own rhyme is now as important on a celebrity's CV as a spell in rehab – although James Blunt, Brad Pitt, Sigourney Weaver and Samantha Janus might prefer to have been overlooked.

For rhyming slang owes little to political correctness. The emphasis is on body parts, diseases and bodily functions with the result that you will find plenty of alternatives for 'arse', 'pox' and 'fart' but nothing much for 'algebra', 'calculus' or 'quantum physics'.

The Ultimate Cockney Geezer's Guide to Rhyming Slang contains over 1,700 rhymes – old and new, popular and obscure – and like any self-respecting dictionary has translations from Cockney to English and vice versa. So if you want to know the contributions that such diverse characters as Nobby Stiles, Vera Lynn and J. Arthur Rank have made to the language, the meaning of quaint phrases like 'Oi Jimmy Knacker', 'tumble down the sink' and 'touch me on the knob', and what Jonathan Ross and Kate Moss, Tony Blair and Rupert Bear or Ray Mears and Britney Spears have in common, the answers are all in this, the ultimate Captain Hook about Chitty Chitty Bang Bang.

Geoff Tibballs

RHYMING SLANG – ENGLISH

A

Abergavenny penny

Ace of spades AIDS

Acid trip rip

Acker Bilk milk
(Somerset-born jazz clarinettist popular in the 1960s and famed for his goatee beard, bowler hat and waistcoat. He was born Bernard Stanley Bilk, his nickname of 'Acker' being Somerset slang for 'mate'. Now he's graduated to Cockney slang, as in, 'Do you want any Acker in your Rosie?')

Adam and Eve believe
(One of the most familiar rhyming slang terms, dating from the late nineteenth century, as in, 'Would you Adam and Eve it, he's run off with my skin and blister!')

Adam Ants pants
(As in, 'Do you fancy that sexy-looking Richard in the leather Adam Ants?')

Adrian Chiles piles
(From the ubiquitous and presumably piles-free TV presenter.)

Adrian Mole dole
(After Sue Townsend's model of teenage angst from the 1980s, as in, 'I got the tin tack at work so it's back on the Adrian again.')

Aesop's Fable bus timetable
(An appropriate rhyme because, like the celebrated stories of the Greek writer Aesop (620–560 BC), bus timetables are complete works of fiction.)

After Eight mint skint
(Usually reduced to 'After Eight', the phrase caught on following the introduction of the chocolate-covered after-dinner mint by Rowntree in 1962.)

Ain't it a treat street

Air Force sauce

Air gunner stunner

Airs and graces Epsom races, braces
(In the 1900s this term referred to Epsom races but it subsequently changed to mean the elastic straps that held up men's trousers.)

Ajax tax
(From the powerful household cleaner introduced in 1947 with the slogan 'Stronger than dirt'. As early as 1948 the American jingle for the product hinted at the future rhyme – 'You'll stop paying the elbow tax/When you start cleaning with Ajax.')

Alan Knott hot
(The former Kent and England wicketkeeper who was hot behind the stumps in the 1970s.)

Alan Ladd sad
(Alan Ladd (1913–64) was a Hollywood tough-guy actor who made a career out of being moody. At a generous estimate of 5ft 5in, he was famously short and had to film many scenes standing on a box or with his leading lady standing in a trench. Perhaps that's why he was sad.)

Alan Minter printer
(Former world middleweight boxing champion and one of Crawley's most famous sons. But he never worked as a printer.)

Alan Whickers knickers
(A much-impersonated British TV personality popular from the 1960s to the 1980s, famous for his travel shows and for

being lampooned on *Monty Python*'s 'Whicker Island'. In rhyming slang the term is usually shortened to 'Alans', as in the 1998 film *Lock, Stock and Two Smoking Barrels* when Nick the Greek says: 'Alright, alright, keep your Alans on!')

Alderman's nail tail
(As in the expression 'as happy as a dog with two aldermen'.)

Alexander the Great plate
(The king of Macedonia (356–323 BC) who spectacularly expanded his empire during his short life.)

Alexei Sayle email
(A modern rhyme based on the Liverpool-born performer who in the 1980s was England's undisputed number one Marxist comedian.)

Alf Garnett barnet (hair)
(An example of rhyming slang once removed with Johnny Speight's foul-mouthed East End bigot from the 1966 sitcom *Till Death Us Do Part* representing 'barnet', which is itself rhyming slang for hair (see **Barnet Fair**). Ironically Alf himself was no more hirsute than the average coot.)

Alfie Moon soon
(A twenty-first-century addition in honour of the chirpy Cockney barman played by Shane Richie in *EastEnders*.)

Alfred the Great weight
(An interesting association since the ninth-century King of Wessex was more adept at burning cakes than calories.)

Ali MacGraw score
(American actress who scored a major success in 1970 with *Love Story*.)

All afloat coat
(A common nineteenth-century term but now obsolete.)

Allan Border out of order
(The rhyme may stem from the former Australian cricket captain's combative leadership and his team's tendency to unnerve the opposition with sledging, which was seen as 'out of order' by the game's traditionalists.)

Alligator later
(Although the phrase 'see you later, alligator' – with its response of 'in a while, crocodile' – was already in use, it really caught on among teenagers after Bill Haley and his Comets had a 1956 hit with the song of that title.)

Almond rock cock (penis)
(Inspired by almond-flavoured sweet rock, which was much sought after by day trippers to the seaside in the nineteenth century. The rhyme is strongly suggestive of oral sex.)

Almond rocks socks

Alphonse ponce (pimp)
(The name implies that only foreigners were involved in such dubious activities and came into use during the Second World War when Londoners understandably viewed outsiders with great suspicion.)

Amsterdam jam
(Usually shortened to 'Amster', which must have convinced visitors to the capital that Londoners regularly ate small furry rodents between two slices of bread.)

Anchor Spreadable incredible
(A butter-based spread from the Anchor company that was labelled 'incredible' because it could be spread direct from the fridge. So listen for John Motson telling the world: 'What a comeback by Chelsea – absolutely Anchor Spreadable.')

Ancient Greek freak

Andrea Corr door
(After the singer with Irish folk-rock band The Corrs.)

Andy Cain rain
(In the past characters were often invented to act as suitable rhymes; Andy Cain was based on no one in particular.)

Andy Capp crap (shit)
(From the *Daily Mirror* strip cartoon created by Reg Smythe in 1956. With his cloth cap welded to his head, Andy was supposed to represent the working man but spent his time assiduously avoiding all forms of work. Instead he guzzled beer at the pub with his mates or lazed on the sofa, leaving long-suffering wife Florrie to listen to his crap... which is why the rhyming slang is quite apt.)

Andy McGinn chin
(Another invented character, the rhyme being in use from the 1930s to the 1950s.)

Andy McNab cab (taxi)
(Pseudonym of the SAS member turned best-selling author who first made headlines with his 1993 book *Bravo Two Zero*.)

Andy Pandy shandy
(First appearing in 1950, stringed puppet Andy Pandy went on to fill the Tuesday slot in *Watch With Mother* to the delight of thousands of pre-school children. Leaving aside his dubious dress sense (what would Trinny and Susannah have made of that blue and white striped shellsuit with matching hat?) and the assignations with Teddy and Looby Loo in the basket, Andy became a cultural icon. Most children attributed his staggering walk to his strings but maybe it was because he had been at the shandy. (See also **Looby Loos**.))

Angus Deayton cheating
(In 2002 lurid tabloid allegations of his adulterous affair with a prostitute led to Deayton's exit as presenter of *Have I Got News For You*, thus making the man once known as 'TV's Mr Sex' synonymous with cheating.)

Anna Maria fire
(Pronounced 'Mareye-ah' rather than 'Mar-ear', this term was popular in the nineteenth century.)

Anna May Wong pong
(The first Chinese American actress to crack Hollywood, Anna May Wong (1907–61) was at the height of her fame in the 1920s and 1930s.)

Anneka Rice price
(A rhyme from the 1980s when Anneka Rice and her fabled bottom were rarely off TV.)

Ant 'n' Decs oral sex
(From chirpy duo Ant McPartlin and Declan Donnelly, in honour of just about the only form of Saturday night entertainment they have yet to present on TV.)

Anthea Turner earner
(Once the golden girl of breakfast TV and *Blue Peter*, where her model of Tracy Island from papier mâché and yoghurt pots transformed the lives of a generation, Anthea has reinvented herself as a domestic goddess, instructing viewers on how to dust properly. It's a far cry from her days introducing Bros on *Top of the Pops*, but it still brings in the money. So a 'nice little Anthea' is quite appropriate – unless you're Eamonn Holmes who once cruelly derided her as 'Princess Tippytoes'.)

Apple fritter bitter (beer)

Apple pips lips

Apple tart fart

Apples and pears stairs
(As in, 'I'm going up the apples to Uncle Ted.' The phrase 'apples and pears' has its origins in the nineteenth century when market-stall holders and barrow boys would arrange their fruit in steps or stairs to attract customers (the shiniest apples and pears at the front), a practice that still continues today.)

April Fools tools, football pools
(This was originally an underworld term for a burglar's tools but it was later extended to embrace the craze for doing the football pools that took off in Britain in the 1930s.)

April showers flowers
(This probably stems from the verse 'April showers bring forth May flowers'.)

Arabian Nights shites
(As in, 'I reckon it was that last pint of Uri Geller gave me the Arabians.')

Aristotle bottle
(This late nineteenth-century term was often condensed to 'arry' and subsequently 'arris', the latter eventually becoming slang for 'arse', partly because of its similar sound but also because of its connection to 'bottle and glass' (see **Bottle and glass** and **Rolf Harris**).)

Armitage Shank bank
(From toilet manufacturers Armitage Shanks, founded in Armitage, Staffordshire, by Thomas Bond in 1817.)

Army and Navy gravy

Artful Dodger lodger, todger (penis)
(As in, 'I've heard the Artful's got an eight-inch Artful.' In use from the mid-nineteenth century – Dickens wrote *Oliver Twist* in 1837 – when lodgers were generally subjected to either innuendo or suspicion.)

Arthur Ashe cash
(Popular with second-hand car dealers, this rhyme is based on black American tennis player Arthur Ashe (1943–93) who was Wimbledon men's singles champion in 1975.)

Arthur Bliss piss
(British composer (1891–1975) who was sometimes referred

to as 'Arthur Piss' by music journalist and fellow composer Kaikhosru Shapurji Sorabji.)

Arthur Daley Old Bailey
(A 1980s rhyme acknowledging the remarkable ability of the dodgy hero of the TV series *Minder* to stay out of the Central Criminal Court.)

Arthur Fowler growler (vagina)
(When *EastEnders'* Arthur Fowler suffered a nervous break-down, it was attributed to money worries but it could well have been caused by an unexpected glimpse of Pauline's growler.)

Arthur Scargill gargle
(The gargle associated with the militant miners' leader is beer rather than mouthwash, as in, 'I'm just nipping down the pub for a quick Arthur with Jim.' On no account should this be confused with a quick J. Arthur (see **J. Arthur Rank**).)

Artichoke ripe pipe
(The reasoning being that if you smoked too much you were liable to suffer from an 'earty choke.)

Ascot races braces
(Usually shortened to 'Ascots'.)

Ashley Cole own goal
(This derives from own goals the England footballer has scored in his private life rather than on the pitch – in particular his autobiography, in which he complained about being offered only £55,000 a week by Arsenal, and the tabloid allegations that he played away from home while married to Girls Aloud singer Cheryl Tweedy.)

Atomic Kitten smitten
(A twenty-first-century rhyme after the English girl band, though it's hard to know who exactly was smitten by them.)

Attila the Hun a 2:1 degree result
(The fearsome king of the Huns (406–453) who died on his

wedding night is fondly remembered by students, as in, 'Congratulations on getting an Attila; I only got a Desmond.')

Auntie Ella umbrella

Auntie Nelly belly

Austin Powers showers
(It would be nice to report that this piece of rhyming slang led to 'power shower' but the term was in existence long before Mike Myers's sex-crazed secret agent tried to save the world from Dr Evil.)

Axl Rose nose
(After the singer with US rock band Guns N' Roses whose stage name (his real name is William Rose) is an anagram of 'oral sex'.)

Ayrton Senna tenner
(Three times Formula One world champion, the charismatic Brazilian racing driver (1960–94) was worth an estimated $400 million at the time of his death in a crash at Imola. So an 'Ayrton' was actually worth a lot more than a tenner. Sometimes it is corrupted to 'dead Brazilian', as in, 'I'll 'ave you know I paid a dead Brazilian for that Peckham.')

B

Baa lamb tram
(Electric baa lambs ran in London from 1901 to 1952 before being reintroduced in Croydon in 2000.)

Babbling brook cook, crook
(First used in First World War military circles to mean 'cook', where it was often shortened to 'babbler'. Between the 1920s and the 1960s, 'babbling brook' enjoyed limited use as a term for 'crook'.)

Baby's pram jam

Bacardi Breezer freezer

Backseat driver skiver
(A neat piece of rhyming slang, since a backseat driver is often perceived as lazy, issuing orders on how to drive while not having the responsibility of the steering wheel.)

Bacon and eggs legs

Bacon bonce nonce

Bacon rind mind

Baden-Powell trowel
(From Sir Robert Baden-Powell (1857–1941), founder of the Boy Scout movement and one of the heroes of the defence of Mafeking in 1900.)

Bag of sand grand (£1,000)
(In vogue during the boom times for City of London traders in the 1980s when their salaries increased by several grand. Then along came Black Monday – 19 October 1987 – and

many yuppie whizzkids proved to be worth little more than an ordinary bag of sand.)

Bag of yeast priest

Baked bean Queen (Elizabeth II)

Baked beans jeans
(Jeans were originally worn principally by cowboys, so this rhyme dating from the 1960s might spring from the association between a cowboy's favourite clothing and his favourite food.)

Baker's dozen cousin
(The term 'baker's dozen' originates from the practice of medieval English bakers adding an extra loaf when selling a dozen in order to avoid being fined, pilloried or flogged under the terms of the Assize of Bread and Ale for giving short measure. Perhaps it was first applied to 'cousin' by someone who came from a relatively large family, with thirteen cousins. The rhyming slang dates from the late nineteenth century.)

Bald head red (snooker ball)
(Applied to the red ball in snooker, even though a bald head looks more like the pink.)

Ball and bat hat
(Popular in England before 1914, after which it was largely replaced by 'Tit for tat'.)

Ball of chalk walk

Ball of lead head
(Used in the British army during the First World War but now obsolete.)

Ballet dancer chancer
(The average Cockney geezer would actually be more suspicious of a male ballet dancer than he would of a risk-taker.)

Balloon car saloon bar

Ballroom Blitz tits
(A phrase that gained in popularity after glam rock band
The Sweet's 1973 hit 'Ballroom Blitz'.)

Balmy breeze cheese

Banana fritter shitter (anus)

Banana splits shits

Band of Hope soap
(The Band of Hope was a British temperance society formed
in Leeds in 1847 to educate children on the perils of drink.
Being advocates of clean living, its members must have used
plenty of soap.)

Bang and biff syph (syphilis)
(Appropriately the phrase suggests a certain carelessness as
to the consequences.)

Bangers and mash cash, slash (urinate)

Bar of soap Pope

Barb wired tired

Barclays Bank wank

Bargain Hunt cunt
(The daytime TV antiques show that made a celebrity out of
the permatanned David Dickinson with his quaint catchphrases 'cheap as chips' and 'bobby dazzler'.)

Barge and tug mug (drinking)

Bark and growl trowel

Barnaby Rudge judge
(A historical novel by Charles Dickens, published in 1841
and dealing in part with the pitfalls of capital punishment.

A judge is referred to in the story but is not one of the principal characters. (See also **Dolly Varden**.))

Barnet Fair hair
(The history of Barnet Fair dates back to 1588 when Queen Elizabeth I granted a charter to the Lord of the Manor of Barnet, Charles Butler, for the staging of a twice-yearly fair. Although essentially a horse fair – races were held on the last three days during the eighteenth century – it also sold livestock and in 1834 was hailed as the largest cattle market in England. Today it is an annual event and primarily a funfair, although a few horses are still for sale. Like much Cockney rhyming slang, the term, which was initially recorded in the 1850s, has entered popular usage in the form of the first word only – 'barnet'. (See also **Alf Garnett**.))

Barney McGrew screw (sexual)
(Along with Pugh, Pugh, Cuthbert, Dibble and Grubb, Barney McGrew was a member of the formidable *Trumpton* fire brigade under the command of Captain Flack in the 1960s children's TV series. Although not widely used, this piece of slang brings a whole new meaning to 'having a barney'.)

Barney Rubble trouble
(Although the meaning is similar, neither is there any connection between Fred Flintstone's pal and the long-standing 'barney' meaning a fight.)

Barry McGuigan big 'un
(In fact the former Irish world boxing champion was quite a small 'un, being a featherweight, but perhaps he packs a punch in his trunks.)

Barry White shite
(After the heavyweight US soul singer (1944–2003), dubbed the 'Walrus of Love'.)

Basil Brush thrush (genital complaint)
(The puppet fox created by Ivan Owen in the 1960s may have come to be linked with a genital complaint because

'brush' is not only a fox's tail but also one of the many slang terms for female pubic hair.)

Basil Fawlty Balti
(Given his contempt for all things foreign, it is hard to imagine the manic Torquay hotelier played by John Cleese in the classic 1970s sitcom *Fawlty Towers* embracing Indian-style cuisine – even if the duck was off.)

Bat and wicket ticket

Bath bun son, sun

Battle cruiser boozer (pub)
(First heard in the 1940s. Barfly Jack, a character in the 1998 gangster film *Lock, Stock and Two Smoking Barrels*, says of an acquaintance: 'He's gone down the battle cruiser to watch the end of a football game.')

Battle of Waterloo stew
(The Duke of Wellington's finest hour certainly left Napoleon in a stew.)

Beano and Dandy shandy
(The use of two children's comics in the rhyme underlines the belief that shandy is not a drink for real men.)

Beans on toast post

Bear's paw saw

Beattie and Babs crabs (pubic lice)
(Beattie and Babs were popular music-hall entertainers who probably weren't itching to be associated with an embarrassing complaint.)

Beecham's Pill still (photograph)
(Originally invented as a cure-all by Thomas Beecham around 1842, Beecham's Pills were a mix of aloe, ginger and soap and were considered one of the most effective laxatives of their day. Their reputation was enough to inspire the

muse in Scotsman William McGonagall, generally considered to be the world's worst poet: 'No matter what may be your bodily ills, the safest and quickest cure is Beecham's Pills.' Their manufacture was finally discontinued in 1998.)

Bees and honey money
(First recorded in 1892, the phrase may be comparing the industry of bees and humans, i.e. bees work hard to produce honey and if humans work hard, they earn money. And in both cases the end result is sweet.)

Bees' wax tax

Beggar boy's ass bottle of Bass (beer)

Beggar My Neighbour on the labour (exchange)
(Also known as Strip Jack Naked, the card game Beggar My Neighbour dates back to at least the mid-nineteenth century, having appeared in Charles Dickens's *Great Expectations* (1861) in which the hero Pip writes: 'I played the game to an end with Estella, and she beggared me.' In rhyming slang, 'on the labour' or 'on the dole' was expressed as being 'on the beggar'.)

Belinda Carlisles piles
(After the US singer, formerly with 1980s all-girl band The Go-Gos, but who subsequently enjoyed piles of hits as a solo artist.)

Bell ringers fingers

Benny Hill till, drill
(The association with 'till' is particularly fitting as comedian Benny Hill (1926–92) was famously careful with money, living in decidedly modest surroundings despite being worth millions.)

Berkshire Hunt cunt
(Hence the abbreviation 'berk', although today this generally carries the less offensive meaning of 'fool' or 'idiot'.)

Berlin Walls balls (testicles)

Bernhard Langer banger (sausage)
(With Germans being so fond of their *bratwurst*, the Bavarian-born former Ryder Cup golfer is a sound choice to represent the noble sausage.)

Bernie Flint skint
(An alternative to 'boracic lint' from the mid-1970s when singer/guitarist Bernie Flint, a former sailor from Southport, won the ITV talent show *Opportunity Knocks* a record twelve times, beating off stiff competition from tap-dancing grannies and singing dogs.)

Bessie Braddock haddock
(A former Labour MP for a Liverpool constituency, Bessie Braddock (1899–1970) was a big name in English politics after the Second World War. Her reputation was matched by her waistline, which suggested that she was no stranger to her local chippy.)

Bethnal Greens jeans
(From the area of East London, as in, 'Isn't it about time you bought a new pair of Bethnals?')

Betty Grable table
(US film star Betty Grable (1916–73) was famed for her shapely legs, which were insured for one million dollars. Even the most ornate table legs would have struggled to compete.)

Beyoncé Knowles sausage rolls
(After the American R&B singer, formerly with Destiny's Child. (See also **Darling Beyoncé**.))

Biffo the Bear hair
(Biffo the Bear made his debut in the *Beano* comic in 1948 and occupied the front cover until 1974 when in a bloody coup he was ousted by Dennis the Menace. As the world's only famous Biffo, the rhyme is easily abbreviated, as in, 'I won't be long, I'm off to get me Biffo cut.')

Big bass drum bum (bottom)
(Sadly with some people the physical similarities alluded to here are all too apparent.)

Big Ben ten

Big dippers slippers
(As in, 'Blow me, the London fog's chewed me big dippers!')

Big Ears and Noddy body
(Big Ears the bearded gnome and Noddy, the boy with a wooden body whose head is on a spring, were created by English writer Enid Blyton and first appeared in print in 1949. Despite their international success, political correctness has reared its ugly head in Toyland. Mr Golly, who ran the garage, was made redundant, the BBC introduced Dinah Doll as 'a black, assertive minority female' for the 1990s TV series, and Big Ears was renamed 'Whitebeard' to avoid drawing attention to his most prominent features. (See also **Clodhopper**.))

Big Mac sack
(McDonald's Big Mac was invented in 1968. It was originally going to be called either the Aristocrat or the Blue Ribbon Burger, neither of which would have rhymed half as well with 'sack'.)

Bill and Ben ten, yen
('Bill and Ben' was originally used to denote the number ten until London City traders of the 1990s expanded its meaning to incorporate the Japanese currency. With their 'flibadobs' and 'flobadobs', Bill and Ben the Flowerpot Men were big hitters in 1950s children's television. Why did they talk funny? Perhaps they smoked a Little Weed.)

Bill Oddie and Ben voddie (vodka)
(A voddie for a Goodie.)

Bill Stickers knickers
(Everyone's favourite victim from the omnipresent warning on walls or hoardings: 'Bill Stickers will be prosecuted.')

Bill Wyman hymen
(A 1980s rhyme inspired by salacious stories about the former Rolling Stone's many sexual conquests. During just two years in the sixties he apparently calculated that he had slept with 278 women.)

Billie Pipers windscreen wipers
(A modern rhyme for the teenage pop star who won a whole new audience as Doctor Who's sidekick Rose Tyler.)

Billy Bragg slag
(After the Essex born singer/songwriter.)

Billy Bunter punter
(Created by Frank Richards, Billy Bunter of Greyfriars School was a popular character in the boys' weekly magazine *The Magnet*, which was published from 1908 to 1940. Nicknamed the 'Fat Owl of the Remove', the overweight schoolboy spent too much time in the tuck shop to bet on horses.)

Billy Button mutton
(The rhyme first appeared in the nineteenth century when 'Billy Button' was slang for an itinerant tailor but drifted out of fashion in the twentieth century as mutton largely disappeared from the British menu.)

Billy Liar tyre
(The title of a 1959 novel by Keith Waterhouse, the story of 19-year-old undertaker's clerk Billy Fisher and his Walter Mitty-like fantasies.)

Billy Ocean suntan lotion
(After the Trinidad-born R&B singer, real name Les Charles.)

Billy Ray Cyrus virus
(He had a 1992 hit with that line-dancing favourite 'Achy Breaky Heart', a condition almost certainly not caused by a virus.)

Billy Smart fart
(Named after the British circus proprietor (1893–1966) whose acts sadly never included the celebrated French farteur Joseph Pujol (aka Le Pétomane) who could anally blow out a candle several yards away.)

Bin lid quid (£1)

Binnie Hale tale
(A conman's yarn, named after actress Binnie Hale (1899–1984), a star of the London stage between the wars.)

Birdlime time (prison sentence)
(Originating in the 1850s, it had been contracted to 'bird' by the 1920s. Hence the term 'to do bird' meaning 'to serve a prison sentence'.)

Bird's nest chest
(No doubt because a hairy chest resembles something that a sparrow has built.)

Biscuits and cheese knees

Black & Decker pecker (penis)
(Since Black & Decker are noted for their mighty tools, it follows that their name would be used as rhyming slang for a penis.)

Black and white night

Black Maria fire
('Black Maria' was first heard in nineteenth-century America to describe a police van carrying prisoners. The term later crossed the Atlantic and entered rhyming slang for the type of fire that required attention from a different branch of the emergency services.)

Blackadder ladder
(After Rowan Atkinson's social climber in the historical TV comedy that ran from 1983 to 1989.)

Blackpool rock cock (penis)
(Inspired by George Formby's 1937 song 'With My Little Stick Of Blackpool Rock', a ditty rife with innuendo.)

Blackpool Tower shower
(From the 518ft tall Lancashire tower (inspired by Paris's Eiffel Tower) that was completed in 1894.)

Blackwall Tunnel funnel
(After the tunnel under the Thames that opened in 1897. Seven people were killed during its construction.)

Blade of grass arse

Blindman's buff snuff
(Blindman's buff is a children's game that dates back 2,000 years to Greece. In Germany it is called 'blind cow'.)

Bloody Mary scary
(Catholic Queen Mary I, who ruled England from 1553 to 1558, earned the nickname 'Bloody Mary' for her ruthless persecution of Protestants. She has inspired a drink and a legend, the latter stating that chanting 'Bloody Mary' thirteen times in front of a candlelit mirror will summon a vengeful spirit... which is pretty scary.)

Blue moon spoon

Bo Diddley tiddly
(After the American blues singer (1928–2008), as in, 'No more Vera for me, I'm feeling Keira Knightley Bo Diddley.')

Bo Peep sleep
(From the nursery rhyme character Little Bo Peep, who was so worried about losing her sheep that she probably found it hard to get to sleep.)

Board and plank Yank

Boat and oar whore

Boat Race face
(The University Boat Race was first staged in 1829 but it was not until after the Second World War that the term caught on as an expression for 'face', usually referring to the sort of countenance that appeared to have been slapped by an oar 30 times a minute. The 1979 hit by The Monks, 'Nice Legs, Shame About The Face', included the line 'nice legs, shame about the boat race'.)

Bob Beamon semen
(The American long jumper's incredible leap at the 1968 Mexico Olympics stood as a world record for 23 years and somehow epitomised male achievement, even though not many sperm can manage a jump of 29ft 2in.)

Bob Cryer liar
(An ironic rhyming slang phrase as Sergeant Bob Cryer was a long-serving character in the TV police series *The Bill* and was renowned for his honesty and for doing everything by the book.)

Bob Dylan villain
(After the iconic US folk singer who sprang to fame in the 1960s.)

Bob Hope dope (cannabis), soap
(The name of the British-born US comedian (1903–2003) was first applied to cannabis in the 1960s, as in, 'Do you know where we can get some Bob Hope?')

Bob Marley charlie (cocaine)
(Based on the Jamaican reggae artist (1945–81) whose views on cocaine are not known but everyone knows he liked his doughnuts wi' jammin'.)

Bobby Moore score (£20)
(England's World Cup-winning captain of 1966 didn't often score – just 28 goals in 807 appearances. That explains why his fellow East Enders put his name to the slang term for £20 instead.)

Bodie and Doyle boil (spot)
(Played by Lewis Collins and Martin Shaw respectively, crimefighters William Bodie and Ray Doyle were characters in the ITV series *The Professionals*, which ran from 1977 to 1983. Bodie did a neat line in safari jackets while Doyle sported the sort of seventies perm much favoured by footballers of that era.)

Boiled beef and carrot claret (blood)
(In boxing 'claret' is a slang term for 'blood', and in rhyming slang that becomes 'boiled beef and carrot' after the Cockney music-hall song 'Boiled Beef And Carrots', which was published in 1909 and performed regularly by Harry Champion (1866–1942). (See also **Darby Kelly**.))

Boiler house spouse
(Hence the less than flattering description of 'er indoors as an 'old boiler'.)

Booed and hissed pissed (drunk)

Boots and socks pox

Boracic lint skint
(Boracic lint was a form of medical dressing popular in the nineteenth century. Just the word 'boracic' is sufficient to mean 'penniless'. First recorded in 1959.)

Boris Becker pecker (penis)
(This entered popular usage when details emerged of the German tennis player's sexual fling with Russian model Angela Ermakova in the broom cupboard of a Japanese restaurant in London in 1999.)

Borrow and beg egg
(Used during the Second World War when due to food shortages, eggs could often only be obtained by borrowing or begging.)

Boss Hogg bog (toilet)
(Jefferson Davis 'Boss' Hogg was the greedy commissioner of

Hazzard County in the 1980s TV series *The Dukes of Hazzard*. He wore a white suit, smoked fat cigars and used to eat raw liver every morning, which could explain why his name has come to be associated with the toilet.)

Bottle and glass arse
(This is the origin of the phrase to 'lose your bottle', meaning to shit yourself through fear. (See also **Aristotle**.))

Bottle and stopper copper (police officer)

Bottle of beer ear

Bottle of booze news

Bottle of cola bowler (hat)

Bottle of rum bum (bottom)

Bottle of sauce horse

Bottle of scent bent (gay)
(A self-explanatory rhyme as a bottle of scent reeks of effeminacy.)

Bottle of Scotch watch

Bottle of water daughter

Bottle of wine fine (penalty)

Bottomless pit shit

Boutros Boutros-Ghali charlie (cocaine)
(Egyptian diplomat who served as Secretary-General of the United Nations from 1992 to 1996. So good his parents named him twice.)

Bow and arrow sparrow
('Who Killed Cock Robin?' asked the nursery rhyme, first published in 1744. 'I, said the sparrow, with my bow and arrow.' (See also **Cock linnet** and **Sparrow**.))

Bow and quiver liver

Bowl of fruit suit

Bowl the hoop soup
(A favourite children's pastime in Victorian times – when soup kitchens for the poor were rife – was bowling an iron hoop along the street. The rhyme caught on because of the link between 'soup' and 'bowl'.)

Bowler hat twat (vagina)

Box of toys noise
(A late nineteenth-century rhyme probably inspired by the row made when a child delves into a box full of toys.)

Brace and bit shit

Brad Pitt shit
(When Eartha Kitt's star began to wane in the 1990s, Brad Pitt stepped into the brown stuff as her natural successor. Jennifer Aniston went for a Brad Pitt in 2000 and it lasted five years.)

Brady Bunch lunch
(*The Brady Bunch* was a US sitcom of the early 1970s that regularly overdosed on saccharin. With six kids in the house, the lunch table must have been a busy place.)

Brahms and Liszt pissed
(Named after German composer Johannes Brahms (1833–97) and Hungarian composer Franz Liszt (1811–86). The pair did meet in Hungary in 1853 but the chance of any future friendship was soured when Brahms fell asleep during Liszt's piano recital of *The Sonata*. Brahms continued to be critical of Liszt's works, so it is highly unlikely that they ever became drinking partners. The rhyme is often shortened to just 'Brahms', which would have further infuriated Liszt.)

Bram Stoker choker
(Irish writer (1847–1912) best known for creating Dracula, who in fairness was more a biter than a choker.)

Brandy butter nutter

Brandy snap slap

Brass band hand

Brass nail tail (prostitute)
('Tail' is an old slang word for 'a woman seen as an object of sexual desire', a category that included whores. Consequently 'brass nail' became the rhyming slang although since the 1930s this has been shortened to 'brass'.)

Brass tacks facts
(The phrase 'getting down to brass tacks' was first used in Texas in 1863. It is believed to derive from the practice of nineteenth-century haberdashers who, when selling material, would measure it between brass tacks that were set into the shop counter.)

Bread and butter nutter, gutter

Bread and cheese sneeze

Bread and honey money
('Bread' was first used as slang for 'money' in the 1940s and is also linked to other basic financial expressions, such as 'dough' and 'earning a crust'.)

Bread and jam tram
(A rhyme from the early twentieth century, reflecting the diet of that period.)

Bread and lard hard

Bread knife wife

Brian Clough rough
(After the outspoken football manager Brian Clough (1935–2004).)

Brian O'Linn gin
(A fictitious Irishman associated with drink? Surely not. But this phrase was so widespread in the late nineteenth century that it was often served in the shorter measure 'Brian'.)

Bricks and mortar daughter

Bride and groom broom, room
(It doesn't take a genius to work out which room in the house newlyweds favour.)

Bridget Jones moans
(An apt rhyme for the self-absorbed thirtysomething character created by Helen Fielding in 1995.)

Brighton line nine
(The London to Brighton railway was opened in 1841, and in 1843 a third-class ticket from the capital to the coast cost 3s 6d.)

Brighton Pier queer (gay)
(Brighton is reckoned to be the gay capital of England and Brighton Pier is one of its proudest erections. The town actually has two piers but the older West Pier caught fire in 2003. The pier was gutted, as were the people of Brighton.)

Bristol Cities titties (breasts)
(Taken from the name of the football team, the term 'bristols' (as in 'what a lovely pair of…') was particularly popular in the 1960s and became familiar to fans of the *Carry On* films. In *Carry On Again Doctor* (1969) there was a joke about Bristol's Bouncing Baby Food, and the producers got more mileage from the idea in *Carry On Henry* (1970) by having busty Barbara Windsor play the daughter of the Earl of Bristol.)

Britney Spears beers, tears
(After the troubled US pop princess, as in, 'I didn't mean

what I said about your mother, so don't start turning on the Britneys.')

Brixton riot diet
(From the Brixton riots of 1981 which gave the government food for thought.)

Broken heart fart

Brown Bess yes
('Brown Bess' was the nickname for the British Army's land pattern musket, which was in use from around 1722 to 1838.)

Brown bread dead
(In the 1970s, this replaced 'loaf of bread' as the most common term for 'deceased' (see **Loaf of bread**). It sometimes appears as 'Hovis', i.e. 'Hovis' = 'brown bread' = 'dead'. Elvis has been Hovis for over thirty years.)

Bruce Lee key
(After the US-born martial arts actor (1940–73).)

Bruno N'Gotty totty
(French footballer who has played in England for Bolton Wanderers, Birmingham City and Leicester City.)

Brussel sprout Boy Scout, shout

Bryant and Mays stays
(An old type of corset rhymed with the well-known match manufacturers.)

Bubble and squeak beak (magistrate), Greek, speak
(Just as bubble and squeak is a cheap dish of leftover mashed potato and cabbage, it is equally versatile in rhyming slang. It has been a term for 'Greek' since the nineteenth century, and when singer George Michael adopted the unshaven look in the 1980s, he was called 'the bubble with the stubble'.)

Bubble gum bum

Buck and doe snow

Bucket afloat coat

Bucket and pail jail
(A rhyme that depicts the act of slopping out. Usually shortened to 'bucket'.)

Bugs Bunny money
(The Warner Bros animated rabbit and lifelong nemesis of Elmer Fudd made his debut in 1939. He was voiced originally by Mel Blanc (1908–89) who famously disliked carrots.)

Bull and cow row (argument)
(Dates back to the nineteenth century and suggests matrimonial discord.)

Bulldozer poser

Bumble bee VD (venereal disease)

Bunsen burner nice little earner
(A regular feature of school science lessons, this invention was named after the German chemist Robert Wilhelm Bunsen (1811–99). The rhyming slang could be linked to 'bunce', a common underworld term for 'money' in the nineteenth century and possibly a corruption of 'bonus'. The word had virtually died out by the 1960s, only to enjoy a recent revival.)

Burdett Coutts boots
(Now obsolete, but in honour of philanthropist Baroness Burdett Coutts (1814–1906) who used to hand out free boots to the poor.)

Burlington Bertie thirty
('Burlington Bertie from Bow' was a popular music-hall song written in 1915 by William Hargreaves and often sung by his wife, Ella Shields, while dressed as a man.)

Burnt cinder window

Burton-on-Trent rent

Bushel and peck neck
(A bushel and a peck were old units of measurement, a bushel being eight imperial gallons and a peck equalling approximately nine litres.)

Butcher's hook look
(The double-ended hook used by butchers for hanging up sides of meat entered rhyming slang in the late nineteenth century and has earned such acceptance that it has been shortened to 'butcher's' since the 1930s.)

Buttered bun one

Buttons and bows toes
(From the 1947 Dinah Shore song 'Buttons And Bows', where, too, the title rhymed with 'toes'.)

Parlez-vous Cockney?

He may have been boracic but that's no Rebecca Loos for having his bell ringers in the Benny Hill. No wonder he got the Big Mac – he's nothing more than a tea leaf.

(He may have been skint but that's no excuse for having his fingers in the till. No wonder he got the sack – he's nothing more than a thief.)

C

C & A gay (homosexual)
(The chain of stores was named after the initials of Dutch brothers Clemens and August Brenninkmeijer who founded the company in 1841... and it doesn't take much imagination to work out what the C & A might stand for in this rhyming slang.)

Cab rank bank

Cabman's rests breasts
(In Victorian London 'cabman's rests' were places where a cabbie might take a short break. The rhyming slang version suggests somewhere else he might enjoy resting his head.)

Cadbury's Snack back

Cain and Abel table
(The biblical sons of Adam and Eve. Cain murdered his brother in a fit of jealousy because Abel's burnt offerings of meat were more acceptable at God's table than Cain's gift of fruit.)

Callard & Bowsers trousers
(English confectionery company founded in 1837 and famous for its butterscotch. Usually shortened to 'Callards' in rhyming slang.)

Calvin Klein fine, wine
(So a 'fine wine' would be a 'Calvin Calvin'.)

Camden Town brown (halfpenny)
(In the nineteenth century copper coins were known as 'browns' and it was in the 1850s that the humble halfpenny

was first rhymed with the north London district of Camden Town.)

Camel's hump dump (shit)

Camilla Parker Bowles Rolls (Royce)
(Both are associated with wealth and have given Prince Charles a ride for over thirty years.)

Can of Coke joke

Canal boat Tote

Canary Wharf dwarf
(An ironic rhyme for one of London's tallest buildings, as in *Snow White and the Seven Canaries*.)

Canterbury Tales Wales
(After the collection of stories written by Geoffrey Chaucer in the fourteenth century.)

Cape Horns corns
(Its location at the foot of South America makes 'Cape Horn' an apt choice to rhyme with a chiropody complaint.)

Cape of Good Hope soap

Captain Bligh pie
(From William Bligh, British naval officer and captain of HMS *Bounty*, whose crew mutinied in 1789. He was later appointed Governor of New South Wales.)

Captain Cook look
(Captain James Cook (1728–79) was the Yorkshire-born explorer who claimed the east coast of Australia for Britain and is thus directly responsible for Rolf Harris, Harold Bishop and Skippy.)

Captain Hook book
(The villain of J.M. Barrie's *Peter Pan*.)

Captain Kirk Turk, work
(The captain of the starship *Enterprise* boldly entered the realms of rhyming slang in the 1990s.)

Captain Morgan organ (musical)
(Henry Morgan (1635–88) was a daring Welsh pirate.)

Captain's log bog (toilet)
(A shrewd choice as 'log' is slang for a huge turd – one that is so big you're afraid to flush it without first breaking it into little pieces with the toilet brush.)

Car park nark (police informant)

Cardboard box pox

Carl Rosa poser
(Carl Rosa (1842–89) founded an English opera company. IIe was a bit grand, which could have led to him being considered a poser in some circles. Or perhaps it was simply that his name rhymed.)

Carlo Gatti batty
(Swiss entrepreneur Carlo Gatti (1817–78) was supposedly the first man to make ice cream available to the general public, although that scarcely makes him certifiable. He later moved into music halls.)

Carpets and rugs jugs (tits)

Carving knife wife

Cash and carried married

Castor and Pollux bollocks
(The twin sons of Leda in Greek mythology but better known to horoscope devotees as Gemini the heavenly twins, which suits those who believe that astrology is a load of Castor and Pollux.)

Cat and mouse house

Catherine Tate late
(The comedy actress has recently taken over from Terry
Waite as the principal rhyme for 'late'. But is he bovvered?)

Cats and mice dice

Cecil Gees knees
(Cecil Gee is a chain of menswear shops.)

Centre-half scarf

Chain and locket pocket

Chairman Mao cow
(In vogue from 1966 when *Quotations From Chairman Mao Tse-Tung* – otherwise known as *The Little Red Book* – was published.
It went on to sell 900 million copies worldwide.)

Chalfont St Giles piles
(That a pleasant village in Buckinghamshire has lent its
name to haemorrhoids seems unfair when so many other
places are better qualified to be the arsehole of England.)

Chalk Farm arm
(The area of north London located on the Edgware arm of
the Northern Line.)

Chandelier queer (gay)
(Often abbreviated to 'shandy', so presumably 'half a
shandy' is a diminutive homosexual.)

Charles James Fox box (at the theatre)
(A theatre box has long been known as a 'Charles James' in
memory of Charles James Fox (1749–1806), Whig politician
and Britain's first foreign secretary.)

Charlie Brown clown
(From the 1959 song 'Charlie Brown' by Jerry Leiber and
Mike Stoller, which features the line, 'He's a clown, that
Charlie Brown.' So nothing to do with *Peanuts*.)

Charlie Chan tan
(Author Earl Derr Biggers featured the Honolulu-based Chinese American detective in six novels from 1925 to 1932. Famed for his Confucius-like words of wisdom and his fourteen children, Charlie Chan appeared in over 40 films in the 1930s and 1940s (played in turn by Warner Oland, Sidney Toler and Roland Winters) and then starred in a 1957 British-made TV series, where he was played by J. Carroll Naish.)

Charlie Chester child molester
(Schoolchildren in the 1950s adopted this unfortunate rhyme in honour of the radio comedian 'Cheerful' Charlie Chester (1914–97) who, it must be stressed, led a thoroughly blameless life. At times he must have wished he had stuck with his real name of Cecil Manser.)

Charlie Drakes brakes (on a vehicle)
(Born Charles Springall, diminutive British comedian Charlie Drake (1925–2006) was famous for his slapstick routines, 'Hallo, my darlings' catchphrase and physical resemblance to Mick Hucknall. At the height of his fame in the 1960s, Charlie, who never could put the brakes on his spending, owned fourteen racehorses, a Surrey mansion, two expensive cars and a yacht, and he employed 84 accountants to sort out his finances.)

Charlie Mason basin
(A late nineteenth-century rhyme, usually denoting an excessive amount rather than a porcelain container. 'He's had a Charlie Mason' meant 'He's had a basinful'.)

Charlie Prescott waistcoat
(Like Charlie Mason, nobody knows who Charlie Prescott was but it was a name that rhymed with 'wescot', as 'waistcoat' used to be pronounced. Strangely Labour politician John Prescott has never caught on as Charlie's successor, perhaps because a waistcoat stretched around his ample frame would look worryingly like the lagging on an immersion heater.)

Charlie Pride ride
(A fictional character, not to be confused with US country music singer Charley Pride.)

Charlie Ronce ponce (pimp)
(Another invented name, and one that appeared along with many other examples of Cockney rhyming slang in Ian Dury's 1977 song 'Blackmail Man'.)

Charlie Smirke berk
(Charlie Smirke (1906–93) was a British jockey who won eleven classics, including four Epsom Derbies.)

Charlton Athletic pathetic
(A rhyme no doubt devised by a Crystal Palace or Millwall fan.)

Charm and flattery battery

Chas and Dave shave
(Chas Hodges and Dave Peacock turned Cockney pub culture into a string of hits in the early 1980s, including 'Rabbit', the title of which comes from 'rabbit and pork', Cockney rhyming slang for 'talk' (see **Rabbit and pork**). Their music-hall-style numbers inspired beer adverts and their beloved Tottenham Hotspur, and they seemed to be on *Top of the Pops* more often than Simon Bates, which was no bad thing. And no party of the time was complete without the album *Chas and Dave's Knees Up*. Their own rhyming slang may be seen as ironic, given that they both sported beards.)

Cheddar cheese keys

Cheeky Chappie nappy
(Brighton-born music-hall comedian Max Miller (1894–1963) was known as 'The Cheeky Chappie' on account of his outrageous *double entendres*. When you change a nappy, you dry the cheeks of a baby's bottom, so there is some logic to the rhyming slang.)

Cheerful giver liver
(An ironic rhyme from the 1950s inspired by the biblical
'God loveth a cheerful giver' (2 Corinthians 9:7), because
there's nothing cheery about having a dodgy liver.)

Cheese grater waiter

Cheesy Quaver favour, raver
(Quavers are a potato snack introduced by Walkers in the
1970s. They also come in bacon, prawn cocktail and salt and
vinegar flavours (a tomato ketchup flavour has been discontinued) but none has found favour quite like the original
cheese Quaver.)

Cheggers Plays Pop shop
('Cheggers' is the nickname of Liverpool-born former child
actor Keith Chegwin, whose music show *Cheggers Plays Pop*
was a mainstay of children's television from the late 1970s.
When Chegwin was later revealed to be a recovering
alcoholic, it was mischievously suggested that the title be
changed to *Cheggers Drinks Pop*. (See also **Keith Cheggers**.))

Cheltenham Gold cold
(After steeplechasing's Cheltenham Gold Cup, first run
in 1924.)

Cherie Blair penalty fare
(In January 2000, Cherie Blair was fined £10 for travelling on
a train without a ticket. She boarded a train at Blackfriars,
London, for her journey to Luton, where she fell foul of the
automatic ticket barriers. She claimed that she had not been
able to buy a ticket for her journey because the ticket office
at Blackfriars was closed and she had insufficient cash to use
a machine, which did not accept credit cards.)

Cherry hogs dogs (greyhound racing)
(As in, 'I'm just going off to Walthamstow cherries.' A
'cherry hog' is an old term for a cherry stone.)

Cherry pie lie

Cherry ripe pipe
(From the nineteenth century, when cherrywood pipes were popular.)

Chevy Chase face
('The Ballad of Chevy Chase' commemorated a fifteenth-century skirmish between the Scots and the English in the Cheviot Hills on the border between the two countries. Over 500 years later, the American entertainer born Cornelius Crane Chase was given the nickname 'Chevy' by his grand-mother, a descendant of the Douglas clan who had repelled the English invaders in the Cheviots that day in 1436. Shortened to 'chevy' and sometimes 'chivvy', it entered rhyming slang in the nineteenth century but was superseded by 'Boat Race' in the 1950s (see **Boat Race**).)

Chew the fat chat
(The first known use of the phrase 'chew the fat' occurred in the 1885 book *Life in the Ranks of the British Army in India* by J. Brunlees Patterson, where it was used to describe soldiers grumbling about conditions in the military. From that original association with complaining, 'chew the fat' has broadened to refer to any idle chat, hence its rhyming slang.)

Chicken dinner winner

Chicken oriental mental
(As in, 'I only told him to stop Lord Mayoring and he went chicken oriental!')

Chicken plucker fucker

Chicken's neck cheque

Chimney and soot foot

China plate mate
(As in, 'Good to see you, me old china.' First recorded in the 1880s, it acquired extensive use during the First World War.)

Chip butty nutty

Chips and peas knees

Chitty Chitty Bang Bang Cockney rhyming slang
(Cockney rhyming slang even has a rhyme of its own in the form of the title of the 1964 children's book written by James Bond creator Ian Fleming. The magical flying car in the book and subsequent film was inspired by a series of huge aero-powered racing cars built by Count Louis Zborowski in the 1920s and which were called 'Chitty Chitty Bang Bang'.)

Chocolate éclair prayer
(As in, 'Win the April Fools? You ain't got a chocolate!')

Chocolate fudge judge

Christian Slater later
(After the US actor who was sentenced to three months in jail after becoming involved in a fight at a Los Angeles party in 1997. High on alcohol and drugs, he hid in a stairwell and fought with police officers while reportedly shouting, 'The Germans are coming and they will kill us!')

Christian Ziege eager
(German defender who played for Spurs from 2001 to 2004 and was always eager to get forward.)

Christmas cheer beer

Christopher Lee pee
(The British horror movie actor was chosen solely for his rhyming capabilities, although it would be a brave man to take a pee in a dark churchyard when Dracula was about.)

Cilla Black back
(The Liverpudlian entertainer has been rhymed with 'back' since the 1980s when *Blind Date* heralded the rebirth of her career. The show proved that Cilla could do more than sing, for which we were all grateful.)

Cisco Kid yid
(Created by O. Henry in 1907, the Cisco Kid developed into a jovial Mexican cowboy, most notably played by Duncan Renaldo in a 1950s TV series. His sidekick was Pancho and every episode ended with a corny joke, followed by cries of, 'Oh, Pancho!' 'Oh, Cisco!' For the purposes of rhyming slang, the Cisco Kid was a derogatory reference to an inhabitant of Golders Green as opposed to Mexico.)

Claire Rayners trainers (shoes)
(Popular from the 1980s and somehow fitting that a shoe designed to ensure that your feet aren't in agony should be named after Britain's best-known agony aunt.)

Clark Kent bent (gay)
(Created by Joe Shuster and Jerry Siegel, Superman's secret identity first appeared in *Action Comics* in June 1938. He might lead a double life, but that doesn't make him gay. Anyway, what would Lois say?)

Clement Freuds haemorrhoids
(The broadcaster and former MP has been representing piles for over 30 years, as more recently has his daughter Emma (see **Emma Freuds**).)

Clickety click sixty-six
(First used during the First World War when housie-housie, a forerunner of bingo, was played by the troops.)

Clodhopper copper (police officer)
(This term comes from the oversize boots associated with police officers. It also contains resonances of 'plod', which became a slang term for a particularly slow-witted police officer after Enid Blyton introduced Mr Plod the policeman in her 1949 Noddy stories. Mr Plod would patrol the mean streets of Toyland on his bicycle, striking fear into the most villainous of goblins with his cry of 'Halt, in the name of Plod!' Of course now he's too busy with paperwork. (See also **Big Ears and Noddy**.))

Clothes pegs legs

Coalman's sack black

Coals and coke broke (penniless)

Coat and badge cadge
(First raced in 1715, Doggett's Coat and Badge is the prize awarded to the winner of an annual rowing contest for apprentice Thames watermen held along a four-and-a-half-mile course between London Bridge and Chelsea. The winner used to be able to charge higher fares on the waterways, hence the financial link.)

Coat hanger clanger

Cobbler's awls balls (testicles)
(A cobbler's awl is the pointed hand tool that shoemakers use to pierce holes in leather. Although the term, which first appeared in the nineteenth century, originally referred specifically to testicles, it has since broadened and become less offensive to mean simply rubbish or nonsense. Albert Steptoe was particularly fond of referring to son Harold's ideas as 'a load of old cobblers'.)

Cockaleekie cheeky
(A traditional Scottish soup derived from the custom whereby the losing bird in a cockfight was plucked, dismembered, tossed into a pot with several leeks and stewed for the enjoyment of spectators. The word is cheekier than the practice.)

Cock and hen ten

Cock linnet minute
(Caged song birds such as linnets were popular in Victorian and Edwardian England, hence the line in the Marie Lloyd music-hall song 'My Old Man (Said Follow The Van)' of 'I followed on wiv me old cock linnet'. The pairing of 'linnet' and 'minute' had been used in the nursery rhyme 'Who Killed Cock Robin?' – 'I said the linnet, I'll fetch it in a minute.' (See also **Bow and arrow**.))

Cock sparrow barrow

Cockroach coach
(First heard in the late 1940s when British holidaymakers travelled extensively by coach, although it is not clear whether the insect association referred to the hygiene on board the vehicles or the fact that they crawled along.)

Cocoa say so
(As in, 'Do I fancy Cameron Diaz? I should cocoa!')

Coldstream Guards cards (playing)

Collar and cuff poof

Collar and tie lie (untruth)

Colonel Blimp shrimp
(A cartoon character devised by David Low for the *Evening Standard* in the 1930s, Colonel Blimp was the ultimate pompous, jingoistic Englishman.)

Colonel Gaddafi café
(The leader of Libya since 1969 and a man more accustomed to a Tripoli palace than a greasy spoon off the Balls Pond Road.)

Comedy Dave rave
('Comedy Dave' is the broadcasting name of David Vitty, who has been sidekick to Radio 1 DJ Chris Moyles since 1998. The word 'rave' was first used to describe wild beatnik parties in London in the late 1950s before being applied to all-night, electronic-music dance parties from the 1980s onwards.)

Conan Doyle boil (spot)
(After Sir Arthur Conan Doyle (1859–1930), creator of Sherlock Holmes. The reasoning is elementary, my dear Watson: it rhymes.)

Condoleezza Rice price
(After the US Secretary of State, as in, 'Have you seen the Condi of that handbag?')

Conger eel squeal (inform on)
(As in, 'If I ever find out who congered on me, he's brown bread.')

Constant screamer concertina
(Echoing the painful sound that a concertina can make in the wrong hands.)

Cooking fat cat
(A spoonerism as well as rhyming slang.)

Corn on the cob blow job, job
(As well as describing an ordinary job, this rhyme can refer to oral sex, no doubt inspired by a man watching a woman trying in vain to fit a whole corn on the cob in her mouth.)

Corned beef chief

Corns and bunions onions

Costantino Rocca shocker
(After the Italian Ryder Cup golfer and often applied to his chosen sport, as in, 'I had a terrible round of golf yesterday, couldn't hit a thing – a complete Costantino.')

Cotton wool pull (chat up)
(As in, 'Let's go on the cotton wool tonight for a couple of Thoras.')

Cough and choke smoke
(A piece of rhyming slang that carries a health warning.)

Council gritter shitter (anus)

Council houses trousers

Country cousin dozen

Couple of bob job
(The implication being that if you got a job, you'd earn some money – from the days when 'bob' was slang for 'shilling'.)

Cow and calf half (pint of beer)

Cow & Gate late
(Some say the baby food company took its name from the rhyming slang, i.e. when a woman is late for her period it could well mean she is pregnant. Others point out that the company was originally formed by the Gates family in Guildford in 1771.)

Cream cookie bookie

Cream crackered knackered
(The word 'knackered', meaning 'worn out' or 'exhausted', has been in common usage since around the 1950s. A 'knacker' was an old name for a harness maker but the twentieth-century meaning probably derives from the knacker's yards of the mid-nineteenth century where old, worn-out horses were bought and slaughtered for their meat or hide.)

Cream crackers knackers (testicles)
(The verb 'to knack' also used mean to 'knock' or 'make an abrupt noise', and so castanets were often called knackers. It is but a small leap of the imagination from castanets to testicles.)

Cream puff huff
(A 'cream puff' is a slang term for a gay person or 'poof', so the huff in question is most likely to be a theatrical hissy-fit.)

Cribbage pegs legs

Crispy duck fuck
(A term that became popular with the proliferation of Chinese restaurants in the UK from the 1960s.)

Crown Jewels tools

Crust of bread head

Cuddle and kiss piss

Currant bun son, sun, *Sun* newspaper
(The long-standing rhyming slang for 'son' or 'sun' widened its scope following the launch of the *Sun* newspaper in 1964. When the *Sun*'s owners, News International, launched free internet access via its website in 1999, they traded on the rhyming slang by calling it CurrantBun.com and promised 'Surfin's simply fun using CurrantBun.')

Custard and jelly telly

Custard creams dreams

Cuts and scratches matches
(In the nineteenth century, poor-quality imported safety matches often cut and scratched the side of the box without igniting.)

Cutty Sark loan shark
(Built in 1869, the clipper *Cutty Sark* stands in dry dock at Greenwich, where it is a familiar London landmark despite being badly damaged by fire in 2007. It has been estimated that the cost of repair could be as high as £10 million. Time to visit a loan shark?)

Cynthia Payne stain
(Cynthia Payne hit the headlines in 1978 when she was jailed for eighteen months for running a Streatham brothel, which became known as the 'House of Cyn'. Famously she held parties at which Luncheon Vouchers were given to guests who then exchanged them for services with prostitutes. The charge was £25, which included food, drink and sex. Julie Walters played her in the 1987 film *Personal Services*. Given the nature of Payne's former business, one can only speculate as to what the stain in question might be.)

Cyril Lord bored
(Cyril Lord (1911–84) was a British carpet magnate famous for his 1960s TV commercials, which featured the promise: 'This is luxury you can afford by Cyril Lord.')

D

Dad's Army barmy
(Possibly inspired by the fact that in the Home Guard sitcom *Dad's Army* (1968–77) Captain Mainwaring repeatedly referred to Private Pike as a 'stupid boy'.)

Daffadown dilly silly
(A daffadown dilly was a sixteenth-century name for a daffodil.)

Daft and barmy army

Daily bread head (of family)
(A phrase that became popular in the days when the head of the family was usually the breadwinner.)

Daily Mail ale, tale

Dairy Box pox
(An unromantic rhyme suggesting that a relationship beginning with the gift of a box of chocolates (introduced by Rowntree's in 1936) could end with a reciprocal gift of a dose of the 'Dairy'.)

Daisy roots boots
(First recorded in 1859, the reasoning behind this piece of slang is that daisy roots are notoriously hard to remove – just like heavy working boots. In his 1960 number one 'My Old Man's A Dustman', Lonnie Donegan sang: 'He looks a proper 'nana in his great big hobnail boots/He's got such a job to pull 'em up that he calls 'em daisy roots.')

Dame Judi Dench stench
(It was a cruel mind that first linked the fragrant actress to a vile pong.)

Damon Hill pill
(This term applies to any pill, although the fact that it is rhymed with the former British racing driver might suggest speed.)

Dan Dares flares (trousers)
(Created by Frank Hampson for the *Eagle* comic in 1950, Dan Dare was the ultimate space hero. He was bold and fearless, which everyone had to be to wear 1970s fashions – an era when flares were definitely a sign of distress.)

Dancing bears stairs

Dancing fleas keys

Dangermouse spouse
(Used in the 1980s when ace secret agent Dangermouse (ably assisted by Penfold) fought to save the world from arch enemy Baron Greenback in the children's animated TV series. Dangermouse was voiced by David Jason, a Cockney favourite from the sitcom *Only Fools and Horses* (see also **David Jason**).)

Danny La Rue clue
(After the Irish drag artist entertainer – born Daniel Carroll – as in, 'I haven't got a Danny what you're talking about.')

Darby and Joan phone, alone
(Darby and Joan was first believed to have been coined as a term for an elderly, happily married couple in a poem by English printer Henry Woodfall (c.1686–1747) whose employer John Darby had a wife named Joan. Darby and Joan clubs remain meeting places for senior citizens but their popularity was never matched by the rhyming slang, which, as a representation for phone, always played second fiddle to 'dog and bone'.)

Darby Kelly belly
(First heard in the late nineteenth century and often abbreviated to 'Darby Kel', as in the line from Harry Champion's

song 'Boiled Beef And Carrots', which claims, 'That's the stuff for your Darby Kel, makes you fat and keeps you well.' (See also **Boiled beef and carrot**.))

Darling Beyoncé fiancée
(Another tribute to US recording artist Beyoncé Knowles (see also **Beyoncé Knowles**).)

Darren Day gay (homosexual)
(The serial love rat, as the tabloids used to refer to him, has been accused of many things, but being gay isn't one of them.)

Darren Gough cough
(After the former England fast bowler who in 2005 used his fancy footwork to win TV's *Strictly Come Dancing*.)

Date and plum bum

David Blaine insane
(An apt choice since the American magician and endurance artist must have a screw loose to want to be buried underground in a plastic box for a week, encased in a block of ice for 63 hours, perched on top of a 105ft-high pillar for 35 hours, suspended in a case without food for 44 days or submerged in a water-filled tank for seven days.)

David Gower shower
(This refers to a shower of rain, as opposed to the shower of cricketers that were under his command as England captain in the 1980s.)

David Hockney Cockney
(The artist was actually born in Bradford, which even on a still day is not quite within the sound of Bow Bells.)

David Jason mason
(English comedy actor who hit the big time in the 1980s as the Pride of Peckham, Del Boy Trotter, in the BBC's *Only Fools and Horses*.)

David Mellor Stella (Artois)
(Ordinarily a gap-toothed, Cambridge-educated former Tory MP with a penchant for classical music would be unlikely to be associated with such a symbol of laddism as Stella Artois beer. But in 1992 Mellor was exposed as one of the lads when the tabloids ran a kiss-and-tell story about his affair with occasional actress Antonia de Sancha, including the almost certainly fictitious claim that he had sex with her while wearing his Chelsea strip. Although sales of Chelsea replica shirts plummeted as wives suddenly pictured their husbands as David Mellor, the man himself managed to cash in on his newfound notoriety by carving out a career as a football guru on radio phone-in shows.)

Davina McCalls balls (testicles)
(After the ballsy *Big Brother* presenter, as in, 'Vinnie Jones grabbed Gazza by the Davinas.')

Davy Crockett pocket
(The King of the Wild Frontier (1786–1836) serves as a macho alternative to Lucy Locket.)

Dawson's Creek streak
(This term entered the rhyming slang dictionary in 1998 when Channel 4 began showing *Dawson's Creek*, a US teen drama series set in New England and starring Katie Holmes, later to become Mrs Tom Cruise.)

Day and night light (ale)

Dead loss boss
(Who hasn't had a dead loss for a boss?)

Deep fat fryer liar

Deep in debt bet
(What you will be if you put too much on the wrong horse.)

Deep sea diver fiver

Denis Law saw
(Like a saw, the former Scottish international footballer was invariably the sharpest thing in the box.)

Dental flosser tosser
(As in, 'You've forgotten your passport, Tarquin? You really are a complete dental!')

Desmond (Tutu) 2:2 (degree result)
(The South African clergyman and political activist came to prominence in the 1980s as an opponent of apartheid. He is probably more comfortable lending his name to a second-class degree than to a ballet dancer's skirt.)

Desmond Hackett jacket
(From the noted *Daily Express* sports journalist.)

Desperate Dans cans (headphones)
(The cowboy from Cactusville has been the mainstay of the *Dandy* comic since 1937. He is so tough that he shaves with a blowtorch and used to eat cow pies until he was forced to stop because of mad cow disease. If he owns a pair of cans, he probably listens to Johnny Cash.)

Diamond rocks socks

Diana Dors drawers (knickers)
(Britain's blonde bombshell of the 1950s, actress Diana Dors (1931–84) was an obvious choice to represent knickers despite her apparent reluctance to keep them on. Yet curiously her real surname, Fluck, has not entered rhyming slang.)

Dick Emery memory
(Although he only ever seemed passably amusing back in the 1970s with his string of characters, comedian Dick Emery (1917–83) has been credited as the inspiration for the likes of Harry Enfield, *The Fast Show* and *Little Britain.* So maybe the memory is playing tricks.)

Dick Van Dyke bike
(After the US actor forever remembered for putting on an

awful Cockney accent as Bert the chimney sweep in the 1964 film *Mary Poppins*. Sadly in a 2003 film magazine poll to find the worst movie accent, Van Dyke could only finish second to Sean Connery who nobly kept that 'baritone Highland burr' regardless of whether he was playing an Irish cop (*The Untouchables*), an English king (*Robin Hood: Prince of Thieves*) or a Russian submarine captain (*The Hunt for Red October*).)

Dickory dock clock
(A term taken from the nursery rhyme 'Hickory Dickory Dock', first published in 1744. The origins of the nursery rhyme are uncertain, but may allude to Richard Cromwell's eight-month reign as Lord Protector of England from 1658 to 59.)

Dicky bird word
(A familiar rhyming slang phrase, dating back to at least the 1930s. It is still active today, as in the Paul McCartney song 'She's Given Up Talking', which contains the lines: 'She's given up talking, won't say a word; even in the classroom, not a dicky bird.')

Dicky dirt shirt
(A 'dickey' was used to describe an old shirt as far back as 1781 and today a London shirt manufacturer offers 'the Mae West quality dickie dirts that won't burn a drum roll in your sky rocket.')

Didgeridoo clue
(A didgeridoo is a wind instrument played by the Aborigines of northern Australia – and despite Rolf Harris's best efforts at education, most of us wouldn't have a clue how to get a decent tune out of one.)

Didn't ought port (wine)
(A rhyme mocking a lady's feigned reluctance to accept the offer of another drink.)

Didn't oughta water

Diet Coke joke
(Presumably for light comedy.)

Ding dong song
(Perhaps to describe one of those occasions when two singers seem to be competing rather than performing in harmony, where a duet becomes more of a duel.)

Ding dong bell hell
(From the sixteenth-century nursery rhyme that saw pussy suffer a hellish time in the well until being pulled out by little Tommy Stout. For putting her in, little Johnny Flynn received the Tudor equivalent of an ASBO.)

Dinner plate mate

Dipstick prick (penis)
(Popularised in the 1980s by Del Boy's frequent lament in *Only Fools and Horses* of 'You dipstick, Rodney!')

Dirty beast priest
(A more accurate rhyme than the Catholic Church would like to believe.)

Dirty Den pen
(Played by Leslie Grantham, devious Den Watts was the first landlord of the Queen Vic in *EastEnders*. Having already come back from the dead, he was bumped off for good in 2005.)

Dirty faces laces

Dirty leper pepper

Dirty whore thirty-four
(An entry in the politically incorrect bingo caller's handbook.)

Divine Brown go down (give oral sex)
(After the Hollywood 'sex worker' who was caught giving actor Hugh Grant a $60 blow job in a car on Sunset Boulevard

in 1995. Swallowing her pride, she claimed the money she earned from her subsequent notoriety enabled her to put her children through private school and buy a four-bedroom house.)

Dixie Deans jeans
('Dixie' was the reluctant nickname of footballer William Ralph Dean (1907–80) who acquired legendary status on Merseyside by scoring a record 60 League goals for Everton in one season, 1927–28.)

Do me goods Woods (Woodbines)
(Launched by W. D. & H. O. Wills in the 1880s, Woodbines were a brand of cheap cigarettes that became a staple diet of soldiers during the First World War. The rhyme may not be ironic since in those days it was claimed that cigarettes were actually healthy – presumably in the same way that mustard gas was healthy.)

Doctor and nurse purse

Doctor Crippen dripping (fat)
(After killing his wife in London and then boarding a ship to Canada accompanied by his mistress dressed as a boy, Dr Hawley Harvey Crippen (1862–1910) achieved national infamy by becoming the first murderer to be captured via the new invention of wireless.)

Doctor Legg beg
(Dr Harold Legg, played by Leonard Fenton, was the venerable *EastEnders*' medic who was discussed more often than seen, such as the occasion when elderly Ethel Skinner nearly wet herself after pondering whether to 'get Dr Legg over'.)

Dog and bone phone
(First recorded in 1961, as in, 'Get on the dog and order us a Ruby.')

Dog and pup cup

Dog's knob job
('The dog's bollocks' has been a symbol of excellence since the 1980s, possibly emanating from the fact that dogs appear to derive enormous satisfaction from licking theirs. *Viz* magazine promoted *Viz: The Dog's Bollocks: The Best of Issues 26 to 31*. Here 'dog's knob' fulfils a similar role of approval, as in, 'A nice Sunday roast – that's just the dog's knob.')

Dog's meat feet

Dolly Mixtures pictures (cinema)
(From the bag of mixed candies and jellies that you could safely eat at the cinema without achieving the disruptive noise levels of popcorn.)

Dolly Varden garden
(Dolly Varden was a character in *Barnaby Rudge* by Charles Dickens, thus setting the rhyme in the mid-nineteenth century. (See also **Barnaby Rudge**.))

Don Revie bevy (drink)
(From the former Leeds and England football manager (1927–89) renowned for his dossiers on opposing teams.)

Donald Duck fuck
(After the cantankerous Disney cartoon character introduced in 1934. Note that in Australia 'Donald Duck' is rhyming slang for 'truck', so if you ask for a 'Donald' Down Under, you may not always get the ride you were expecting.)

Donald Trump dump (shit)
(After the US businessman with the dodgy barnet.)

Doner kebab stab

Donkey's ears years
(The 'donkey's ears' rhyme was first recorded in 1916 but made way for the more familiar 'donkey's years' – meaning 'a long time' – in the 1920s. The association with the animal is thought to have originated because a donkey's ears are particularly long.)

Don't make a fuss bus

Doorknob bob (shilling)

Doris Day gay (homosexual)
(From the wholesome US singer and actress who was popular in the 1950s and became a gay icon.)

Dot and dash moustache

Dot Cotton rotten
(Dot Cotton joins Alfie Moon, Arthur Fowler, Dirty Den, Doctor Legg, Ian Beale, Kat Slater and Pat and Frank Butcher in the *EastEnders* hall of Cockney rhyming slang. This is a bit harsh on God-fearing Dorothy, because it was her son Nick who was rotten.)

Doublet and hose nose

Doublet and hosed closed

Douglas Hurd third (degree result), turd
(The former Conservative politician has been given a raw deal in being associated with both a degree that nobody wants and a piece of excrement.)

Dover boat coat

Dover harbour barber

Down the drain brain

Down the hatch match
(The drinking phrase 'down the hatch' was first recorded in 1931 and its celebratory nature mirrors the euphoria felt when your football team has won its match – an occasion that is often marked with a pint or two.)

D'Oyly Carte fart
(An incongruous rhyme taken from the name of the English opera company that specialises in Gilbert and Sullivan, and not to be confused with the 'doily' that is a paper napkin.

Thus a dinner party hostess hearing a Cockney voice proclaim, 'Sorry, I've just dropped a D'Oyly,' should not rush to pick it up.)

Dripping toast mine host (publican)

Drum and fife knife, wife
(A fife is a small flute used in conjunction with a drum in military music.)

Drum roll hole

Dublin trick brick
(Arising from the Irish association with labourers.)

Duchess of Fife wife
(Usually abbreviated to 'Dutch' and immortalised in Albert Chevalier's affectionate1893 song 'My Old Dutch', in which he wrote, 'There ain't a lady living in the land/That I'd swap for me dear old Dutch.')

Duchess of Teck cheque
(Mary Adelaide, Duchess of Teck (1833–97), was a granddaughter of George III and cousin of Queen Victoria.)

Duchess of York pork
(A rhyme that appeared in the 1980s when Sarah Ferguson was less than svelte.)

Duck and dive jive
(Market traders have long been known for their ability to duck and dive – meaning 'to dodge' – so this was a rhyme-in-waiting when the jive dance arrived in the UK in the late 1950s.)

Duck's arse grass (police informant)
(This rhyme entered underworld parlance in the late 1950s when a 'duck's arse' was the name given to a men's hairstyle popular among teddy boys who had their hair swept back along the sides and tapered to a point at the nape so that it resembled a duck's tail feathers.)

Dudley Moores sores
(After the English actor, comedian and musician (1935–2002).)

Duke of Kent bent (gay), rent

Duke of York chalk, fork, talk, walk

Dunlop tyre liar

Dustbin lid kid (child)
(As in, 'Thank God you're home – the dustbins have been playing me up all day.')

Parlez-vous Cockney?

The ole jamjar's off the frog and toad because the Starsky and Hutch keeps slipping, the Billie Pipers are silver and gold, the Shirley Bassey needs repairing, the Tony Slattery's flat and the Charlie Drakes have gone Pete Tong. So it's in the Steve Claridge.

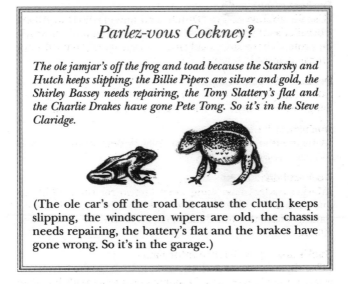

(The ole car's off the road because the clutch keeps slipping, the windscreen wipers are old, the chassis needs repairing, the battery's flat and the brakes have gone wrong. So it's in the garage.)

E

Earls Court salt

Early hours flowers

Early morn horn (erection)
(In acknowledgement of the fact that the average man is standing to attention as soon as he wakes up.)

Eartha Kitt shit
(Names can be so cruel. Whereas a group of Diana Rosses could be an audition for *Stars in Their Eyes*, more than one Eartha Kitt constitutes diarrhoea, as in, 'That Captain Bligh's given me an attack of the Earthas.')

Earwig twig (understand)

East and west chest, vest

East India Docks pox
(After London's Thames-side docks that were built in 1806 and closed in 1967.)

Easter bunny money

Eau de Cologne phone

Eddie Grundies undies (underpants)
(Eddie Grundy is a character in the long-running rural radio serial *The Archers*.)

Edinburgh Fringe minge (female pubic hair)
(In addition to the rhyme there is also the hairy link between 'fringe' and 'minge' – comedy writer Barry Cryer has claimed that the Kenny Everett character Cupid Stunt was originally going to be called Mary Hinge.)

Edmundo Ros boss
(After the Latin American band leader popular in the 1950s.)

Edna Everage beverage
(Barry Humphries created his typical Australian housewife from Moonee Ponds in 1955 before she evolved into a gladioli-loving, acid-tongued, egomaniacal, global superstar.)

Edward Heath teeth
(When he lapsed into one of his shoulder-heaving laughs, former Conservative Prime Minister Heath (1916–2005) always revealed a set of teeth more readily associated with a Grand National winner.)

Egg yolk joke

Eiffel Tower shower

Elephant & Castle arsehole
(From an area of south London, formerly known as Newington, but which adopted the name of the pub on the site from around 1750.)

Elephant's trunk drunk
(As in, 'I was well elephants at that Russell Harty last Saturday.')

Elgin City shitty
(A recent rhyme commemorating one of Scottish football's least successful teams, as in 'That is Allan Border – what an Elgin City thing to do.')

Eliot Ness mess
(A US federal agent based in Chicago, Eliot Ness (1903–57) was the leader of a crack squad – nicknamed 'the Untouchables' – that was responsible for the downfall of mobster Al Capone and others during the government-inspired mess that was known as Prohibition.)

Elizabeth Regina vagina

Elsie Tanner spanner
(Played by Pat Phoenix (1923–86), Elsie Tanner was the siren of Weatherfield who reigned supreme in *Coronation Street* for 23 years.)

Elton John con
(After the flamboyant singer/songwriter.)

Emma Freuds haemorrhoids
(It doesn't need her great-grandfather, psychoanalyst Sigmund Freud, to work out why her name is so often associated with piles. (See also **Clement Freuds**.))

Engelbert Humperdinck drink
(Named after the sixties crooner born Arnold Dorsey rather than the original Engelbert, a nineteenth-century German composer.)

Enoch Powell towel
(From the controversial Conservative MP (1912–98), the towel perhaps being useful for wiping up the 'rivers of blood' that he predicted in his inflammatory 1968 speech about immigration.)

Errol Flynn chin
(In memory of the swashbuckling, extrovert Australian movie star (1909–59), who took everything on the chin.)

Euan Blair Leicester Square
(In 2000, Tony Blair's 16-year-old son Euan was arrested for being drunk and incapable in London's Leicester Square – just a few days after the Prime Minister had proposed on-the-spot fines for drunken and disorderly behaviour. For rhyming slangers, the incident was manna from heaven.)

Evelyn Laye play
(After the British light comedy actress (1900–96) nicknamed 'Boo' who appeared in numerous plays in a long and distinguished career that saw her performing well into her nineties.)

Everton toffee coffee
(Everton toffee was first made in the suburb of Liverpool in the mid-eighteenth century. It first entered rhyming slang in the 1850s, perhaps inspired by the fact that the toffee is made with cream, just as cream is often added to coffee.)

Ewan McGregor beggar
(The Scottish actor shot to fame in the 1996 film of Irvine Welsh's novel *Trainspotting*, playing heroin addict Mark Renton who is reduced to petty theft in order to finance his latest fix while others in his circle of friends resort to begging.)

Eyes front cunt
(From the military command whereby the troops on parade are facing the sergeant major... which would explain the rhyme.)

F

Fag packet jacket

Fainting fits tits (breasts)

False alarm arm

False start fart
(As in, 'I sat down for a Forrest but it was a false start.')

Fanny Blair hair (pubic)

Fanny Cradock haddock
(Unlike Fanny Blair, Fanny Cradock (1909–94) did exist, which is just as well because no writer's imagination could have invented the Cruella de Vil of the kitchen. The cook with the hectoring manner, throaty voice and overblown make-up was a television mainstay of the fifties and sixties until she made the mistake of belittling a member of the public instead of her usual target, husband Johnnie. Given her profession, the rhyme is obvious – indeed a thinly disguised Fanny Haddock was a character in radio's *Beyond Our Ken.*)

Fanny Hill pill (contraceptive)
(The contraceptive pill first became available in Britain in 1961 and two years later the reprint of John Cleland's 1749 novel *The Memoirs of Fanny Hill* was banned for obscenity. So the two events became inextricably linked as part of the Swinging Sixties and the new so-called permissive society … plus there is the obvious association between the pill and 'fanny' (slang for 'vagina').)

Farmer Giles piles
(In his diaries, comedy actor Kenneth Williams complained about suffering from 'the farmers', an alternative to the

Chalfonts (see **Chalfont St Giles**). 'Farmers' itself has also produced a rhyme (see **Judith Chalmers**).)

Fat and wide bride
(The school playground lyrics to Wagner's 'Bridal Chorus' from the opera *Lohengrin* often contain the line, 'Here comes the bride – short, fat and wide.')

Fatboy Slim gym
(After the latest moniker of former Housemartins musician Quentin/Norman Cook. The idea is that you can turn from a fat boy to slim by going to the gym.)

Father Ted dead
(This might seem a cruel rhyme in view of the fact that Irish actor Dermot Morgan, who played Father Ted in the award-winning sitcom, died suddenly in 1998 after the third series, but he would probably have appreciated its black humour.)

Field of wheat street
(Chosen because a field of wheat is the very opposite of a bustling city street.)

Fillet of cod sod

Fillet of plaice face

Fine and dandy brandy

Finger and thumb mum, rum

Fireman's hose nose
(If you can't see the relevance in this rhyme, think anteater or Barry Manilow.)

First-aid blade (knife)
(Another dark rhyme, the former suggesting the results of an attack with the latter.)

First-aid kits tits (breasts)

Fish and tank bank

Fish hook book

Fisherman's daughter water
(Dating from the nineteenth century, as in, 'I'll have a gold watch and fisherman's.')

Fit and spasm orgasm

Five to twos shoes
(Possibly derived from the angle of a person's feet while standing.)

Flea and louse whore house

Fleas and ants pants

Flounder and dab cab

Flowery dell cell (prison)
(An ironic rhyme dating back to the 1920s and usually shortened to 'flowery'.)

Fly a kite shite

Fly-by-nights tights

Fly tipper nipper (child)

Fog and mist pissed
(An indication of the lost sensation that comes from drinking too much.)

Fore and aft daft

Forrest Gump dump (shit)
(A 1986 novel by Winston Groom that became a hit movie in 1994 with Tom Hanks in the title role. Maybe the reason Forrest ran so much was that he was desperate for the toilet.)

Forsyte Saga lager
(A piece of slang inspired by the1967 BBC adaptation of John Galsworthy's novel. It was a wry rhyme because the

show proved so popular that pubs in Britain were actually deserted on Sunday nights during its 26-week run.)

Fortnum & Mason basin
(The up-market Piccadilly department store founded in 1707 and renowned for its luxury food hampers not only gives its name to a mundane container but worse still to a 'pudding-basin' haircut, the sort that barbers with ambitions to be Sweeney Todd used to give schoolboys in the 1950s.)

Four by two Jew
(Sometimes abbreviated to a 'forby'.)

Fox and badger tadger (penis)

Frank and Pat chat
(Frank and Pat Butcher were a married couple on the BBC soap *EastEnders*, although any cosy chats they had were usually conducted through gritted teeth.)

Frank Bough off
(Refers chiefly to food stuffs that are off or past their sell-by date, much as the avuncular *Grandstand* presenter was deemed to be after his sex and drugs scandal hit the tabloids.)

Frank Zappa crapper (toilet)
(After the US rock musician (1940–93), one-time leader of the Mothers of Invention.)

Frankie Dettori story
(A recent rhyme celebrating the effervescent Italian jockey who delights British crowds by performing a flying dismount after riding a Group One race winner.)

Frankie Fraser razor
(After London underworld figure 'Mad' Frankie Fraser who was not averse to using a razor on his victims – that is, when he was not pulling out their teeth with a pair of old pliers.)

Frankie Howerd coward
(Comedian Frankie Howerd (1917–92) might have fitted

the bill by appearing nervous on stage but really he must have been brave to have worn that ginger toupee for decades and think that nobody would notice.)

Frankie Vaughan porn
(In honour of the high-kicking British singer (1928–99), as in, 'Watching all that Frankie Vaughan is ruining my minces.')

Franz Klammer slammer (jail)
(The 'slammer' became slang for 'jail' on account of the cell door being slammed shut behind the inmates at night. Here it is rhymed with the champion Austrian skier of the 1970s.)

Frasier Crane pain
(Played by Kelsey Grammer, the pompous, narcissistic psychiatrist propped up a Boston bar in the popular 1980s US sitcom *Cheers* before moving to Seattle for his own award-winning spin-off, *Frasier*. In terms of being a pain, he was matched only by his equally snobbish brother Niles.)

Fred Astaire hair
(Based on the immaculately groomed US actor and dancer (1899–1987) whose real name was Frederick Austerlitz.)

Friar Tuck fuck
(Rhyming slang incorporating a spoonerism – 'try a fuck' – for Robin Hood's portly companion.)

Fridge freezer geezer

Frog and toad road
(First recorded in the 1850s, usually shortened to 'frog'. The exact origin of the rhyme is unclear but one theory put forward is that in the nineteenth century Londoners could only get to see frogs and toads through travelling by road out into the countryside.)

Frog in the throat boat

Fromage frais gay (homosexual)

Fruit and nuts guts

Fruit Gum chum
(Almost certainly stemming from the 1950s TV commercials for Rowntree's Fruit Gums where a small boy pleaded, 'Don't forget the Fruit Gums, Mum.' Following complaints from parents that they were being unfairly pressurised, the tagline was later changed to 'Don't forget the Fruit Gums, chum.')

Frying pan old man (husband or father)

Fun and frolics bollocks

Funny feeling ceiling

Parlez-vous Cockney?

Let's have a butcher's at the Bruno N'Gotty on page 3 of the Currant Bun. Blimey, what a lovely pair of thrupenny bits – you could get turned and tossed in those!

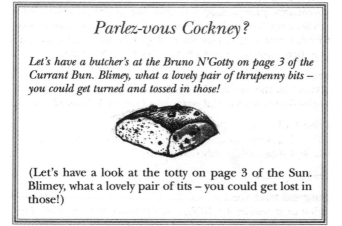

(Let's have a look at the totty on page 3 of the Sun. Blimey, what a lovely pair of tits – you could get lost in those!)

G

Game of nap cap
(Nap – short for Napoleon – was a popular card game around the turn of the twentieth century.)

Garden fence dense
(No doubt arising from the phrase 'thick as two short planks'.)

Garden gate magistrate, eight

Garden gnome comb

Garden plant aunt

Garden tool fool

Gareth Gates masturbates
(After the Bradford-born singer who tasted fame in 2002 by finishing runner-up to Will Young in the ITV talent show *Pop Idol*. His consolation prize was an unlikely affair with pneumatic model Jordan.)

Gareth Hunt cunt
(Somewhat harsh on the *New Avengers* actor (1942–2007), whose only crime against humanity was shaking coffee beans in an inane manner in a 1980s TV commercial for Nescafé.)

Gary Barlow Monte Carlo
(A 1990s rhyme taken from the Take That singer/songwriter.)

Gary Glitter bitter (beer), shitter (anus)
(The time was when people were happy to walk into a pub and ask for 'a pint of Gary', but since his high-profile court case the 1970s pop star's name has taken on a different meaning and he has been relegated to the bowels of civilisation.)

Gary Neville devil
(Many London football fans see the long-serving full back as the very epitome of evil, simply because he plays for Manchester United.)

Gary Player all-dayer (drinking session)
(After the South African golfer still participating in major tournaments in his seventies – his enduring fitness being testimony to a lifetime's abstinence from all-dayers.)

Gates of Rome home

Gay and frisky whisky
(First recorded in the 1920s but unsurprisingly its popularity has declined since 'gay' has acquired a fresh connotation.)

Gay Gordon traffic warden
(Based on the nineteenth-century Scottish country dance called the Gay Gordons.)

General election erection

Geoff Hoon buffoon
(Tony Blair's hapless Defence Minister whose calamities in office during the war in Iraq led to him being christened 'Buff Hoon'.)

Geoff Hurst first (degree result), thirst
(It is only proper that England's hat-trick hero of the 1966 World Cup final should be associated with excellence.)

Geoffrey Chaucer saucer
(After the English poet (1340–1400), author of *The Canterbury Tales.*)

George and Ringo bingo
(There was never much equality in the Beatles. Lennon and McCartney got all the kudos while Harrison and Starr seemed to make up the numbers. Thus John and Paul gave their names to the Pope while George and Ringo had to settle for bingo.)

George and Zippy nippy (cold)
(George and Zippy were characters in the ITV children's series *Rainbow,* which ran from 1972 to 1992, acquiring cult status along the way. George was a shy, rather camp, pink hippopotamus and Zippy was a loud, overbearing, alien-like creature with a zip for a mouth. (See also **Zippy and Bungle**.))

George Bernard Shaw door
(From the name of the Irish playwright (1856–1950), as in the Larry Grayson catchphrase, 'Shut that George Bernard!')

George Blake snake
(An appropriate rhyme for Englishman George Blake (1922–94), who in 1961 was exposed as a double agent and convicted of spying for the Soviet Union.)

George Melly belly
(Named after the ample stomach of the jazzman, broadcaster and general *bon viveur* (1926–2007).)

George Michael menstrual cycle
(A rhyme based on the singer who is unlikely to disrupt anyone's menstrual cycle.)

George Raft draught
(From the American tough-guy movie star (1895–1980), as in, 'Can you feel the George Raft in here?')

Georgie Bests breasts
(Few men were better qualified to judge the merits of the female bosom than George Best (1946–2005), who played football in between dating Miss Worlds.)

Germaine Greer beer
(It was a brave soul who first rhymed the ardent Australian feminist with a singularly male pursuit.)

German band hand
('German band' was the name given to groups of strolling

musicians that used to play in the streets of London and other major cities in the early twentieth century.)

Gerry Cottle bottle
(Named after the aspiring juggler who ran away to join the circus at the age of fifteen in 1961 and was running his own circus within ten years. That took a lot of bottle.)

Gert and Daisy lazy
(Popular Cockney characters from 1930s and 1940s radio created by comedy double act Elsie (1895–1990) and Doris (1904–78) Waters, sisters of Jack Warner (aka Dixon of Dock Green).)

Gertie Gitana banana
(Gertie Gitana (1888–1957) was a music-hall singer from the early twentieth century but is best remembered for possessing one of the few names that rhymes with 'banana'.)

Gianluca Vialli charlie (cocaine)
(After the Italian international footballer who later managed Chelsea (1998–2000) and Watford (2001–02).)

Gilbey's gin chin
(The name 'Gilbey's' has been seen on bottles of gin since 1872, its London dry gin being a particular favourite. This link to the capital probably explains its adoption in rhyming slang.)

Ginger ale jail

Ginger beer queer (gay)
(Dating from the 1920s, and usually just the word 'ginger' is enough to denote 'gay', which is unfortunate for the likes of Mick Hucknall, Chris Evans, Nicholas Witchell and Wilma Flintstone.)

Giorgio Armani sarnie (sandwich)
(Presumably denoting a designer sandwich as opposed to something like cheese and pickle.)

Giraffe laugh
(As in, 'Is he having a giraffe?')

Girl and boy toy

Girls and boys noise
(Probably thought up by someone passing a school playground at break time.)

Give and take cake

Glasgow Ranger stranger
(A supporter of Glasgow Rangers would certainly feel a stranger at Celtic Park, home of their great rivals.)

Glass of beer ear

Glass of plonk conk (nose)

Glenn Hoddle doddle
(From the gifted footballer who found his short reign as England manager anything but a doddle.)

Gloria Gaynors trainers
(It's always hard to throw out a favourite pair of old trainers – the American singer never could say goodbye to hers.)

God almighty nightie
(Presumably the exclamation of the first man who saw Vanessa Feltz in one.)

God forbid kid (child)
(From the early twentieth century and apparently inspired by the lament of an impoverished man at the prospect of yet another mouth to feed.)

Gold watch Scotch (whisky)
(This nineteenth-century rhyme surely stems from the colour of whisky.)

Golden Hind blind
(After the name of the ship in which Sir Francis Drake sailed

around the world between 1577 and 1580, pausing only to relieve Spaniards of their riches.)

Goldie Hawn prawn
(A modern rhyme based on the US comedy actress who first came to prominence on the madcap 1960s TV series *Rowan and Martin's Laugh-In.*)

Goldilocks pox
(A clear warning of the dangers of sleeping with bears.)

Gone to bed dead
(Hearing that her husband's 'gone to bed' must have confused many a Cockney wife, unsure whether to prepare his supper or his funeral.)

Goodie and baddie paddy (Irishman)

Goose's neck cheque

Gooseberry puddin' woman
(A twentieth-century term whereby a man might refer to his wife as his 'old gooseberry'.)

Gordon Brown frown
(Inspired by the concerned expression that suggests he has just lost a 10p piece down the back of his sofa at Number 10 and that days of searching – including bringing in metal detectors and sniffer dogs – have failed to unearth it.)

Gordon the Gopher sofa
(As in, 'Get your plates off the Gordon!' The squeaky glove puppet sidekick of Phillip Schofield on children's TV in the late 1980s, Gordon the Gopher was once attacked by a real dog on the Saturday morning show *Going Live.*)

Gorillas in the Mist pissed
(From the 1988 movie about the work of naturalist Dian Fossey with mountain gorillas in Rwanda. The rhyme is usually condensed to 'gorillas', as in, 'The last time I saw him, he was completely gorillas.')

Grandfather clock cock (penis)
(As in the chat-up line, 'My grandfather would like to meet you.')

Granny's wrinkles winkles

Grape vine clothes line
(Would Marvin Gaye's hit have had the same impact had it been titled 'I Heard It Through The Clothes Line'?)

Grass in the park nark (police informant)
(A rhyme that uses the 1930s term 'grass' for 'informant' (probably from 'snake in the grass') to link up with 'nark', which dates back to the mid-nineteenth century.)

Grasshopper copper (police officer)

Greengages wages
(First recorded in 1931 and often shortened to 'greens', a colour associated with money not least because pound notes were green.)

Greens and brussels muscles
(A rhyme originating from the belief that eating your greens helps build up muscles.)

Gregory Peck cheque, neck
(After the US film actor (1916–2003) and often used colloquially for 'neck', as in, 'Get that down your Gregory.')

Gregory Pecks specs (glasses)

Grey mare fare
(Originating from the days of nineteenth-century horse-drawn transport.)

Growl and grunt cunt
(This term is more anatomical than the likes of 'Gareth Hunt', actually referring to the female vagina as opposed to a random insult. The phrase was shortened in the 1990s to 'growler' and popularised on the Channel 4 TV show *Bo'*

Selecta! in which the Lorraine Kelly character says 'Have you seen me growler?' as she parts her legs to reveal an unsightly mound of pubic hair.)

Grumble and grunt cunt
(Probably inspired by the sounds of rampant love-making, this term has been around since the 1930s and is often used in reference to the actual sex act, as in, 'I've heard his old gooseberry is not averse to a bit o'grumble wiv a Glasgow Ranger.')

Grumble and mutter flutter (bet)

Guinea pig wig

Gypsy's kiss piss
(Rock group Deep Purple used 'Gypsy's Kiss' as the title for a track on their 1984 album *Perfect Strangers*.)

Gypsy's warning morning
(Not exactly an omen for a good day ahead.)

Are you a real fridge freezer?

1. What item of clothing is rhymed with Diana Dors?

2. If someone asked for a blue moon, what would you hand them?

3. Which jockey is the rhyme for 'story'?

4. If you had a drum roll in your Herbie Hides, what would be your problem?

5. If Andy Cain is on the way, why should you fetch Auntie Ella?

6. What ailment is often referred to as 'farmers'?

7. To which part of the anatomy does Boris Becker lend his name?

8. What role is fulfilled by a cheese grater in a restaurant?

9. What nationality is a Bubble?

10. What relation to you is your bricks and mortar?

Answers: 1. Drawers 2. Spoon 3. Frankie Dettori 4. A hole in your strides (trousers) 5. Because it's going to rain so you need an umbrella. 6. Piles (Farmer Giles) 7. Pecker (penis) 8. Waiter 9. Greek (bubble and squeak) 10. Daughter

H

Häagen-Dazs arse
(The upmarket New York ice-cream company founded by
Reuben Mattus in 1961, and from it the expression 'to take
it up the Häagen.')

Haddock and bloater motor

Hail and rain train
(First coined in the 1920s before trains became an endangered species in Britain.)

Hair gel bell

Hairy knees please

Hairy muff fair enough

Hale and hearty party

Hale and Pace face
(After comedians Gareth Hale and Norman Pace, the duo
responsible for 'The Management' and not much else.)

Half a crown brown (snooker ball)
(A half-crown was worth two shillings and sixpence (12½p)
until the coin was discontinued in 1967.)

Half a nicker vicar
(In Cockney slang a 'nicker' was £1, so in old money 'half a
nicker' was ten shillings (or 50p in today's terms). When referring to a member of the clergy, it was usually condensed to
'Arthur', no doubt prompting outsiders to ponder the whereabouts of this gentleman by the name of Arthur Nicker.)

Half and half scarf

Half-inch pinch (steal)
(First recorded in 1925, as in, 'Who's half-inched me half and half?')

Half-ounce bounce (a cheque)
(The common factor in this rhyme is a short measure.)

Half-ouncer bouncer (doorman)

Halfpenny dip ship
(A London dockers' rhyme from the mid-nineteenth century, referring to a lucky dip in a sweet shop where, for the price of a halfpenny, you lowered your hand into a jar or bowl and emerged with sweets.)

Halfpenny stamp tramp
(A rhyme probably taken from the value of the tramp's worldly possessions.)

Ham and cheesy easy

Ham shanks Yanks (Americans)

Hammer and discus whiskers

Hampstead Heath teeth
(Usually shortened to 'Hampsteads', this term was first recorded in 1887.)

Hampton Wick prick (penis)
(Originating in the late nineteenth century, this familiar phrase refers to an area of south-west London and is invariably abbreviated to 'Hampton'. Of course it's even worse if you get your Hampton Court.)

Hand and fist pissed

Hands and feet meat

Hanger Lane pain
(Meaning a 'pain in the neck', which the infamous Hanger Lane gyratory system, introduced in the 1970s, certainly is to

drivers in West London. In 2007 it was named Britain's scariest road junction.)

Hank Marvin starvin'
(Born Brian Robson Rankin, Shadows' guitarist Hank Marvin is famous for owning the first Fender Stratocaster in the UK and for being a Jehovah's Witness. He is easy to spot, not only for his trademark glasses but also because he will be the only caller at your door to combine a deep religious message with the riff from 'Apache'.)

Hannibal Lecter ticket inspector
(The cannibalistic serial killer created by author Thomas Harris and given flesh by Anthony Hopkins in the 1991 film *The Silence of the Lambs* is arguably one of the few people in the world scarier than a ticket inspector.)

Hans Blix fix
(An appropriate rhyme for those who believe that the American and British governments deliberately exaggerated the threat posed by Iraq as an excuse to go to war in 2003, especially after Swedish diplomat Dr Blix, the UN inspector, failed to discover the promised weapons of mass destruction.)

Hansel and Gretel kettle
(The two young heroes of the Brothers Grimm fairy tale cooked the wicked witch in her own oven, but possibly only because she was too big to be boiled in a kettle.)

Hansom cabs crabs (pubic lice)
(The Hansom cab was a horse-drawn carriage designed by Joseph Hansom in 1834. They were a familiar sight on the streets of London until the advent of the motor car in the 1920s.)

Harbour light right

Hard hit shit
(Probably the work of a rhyming slanger with constipation.)

Hard labour neighbour

Hare and hound round (of drinks)

Harold Macmillan villain
(The Conservative politician (1894–1986) was hardly Ronnie Kray, although he did demonstrate his ruthlessness on the so-called 'Night of the Long Knives' in July 1962 when as Prime Minister he sacked seven members of his cabinet.)

Harold Pinter splinter
(From the renowned English playwright.)

Harpers and Queens jeans
(A strange choice since it's unlikely that the women's style magazine *Harpers & Queen* would be required reading in the London street markets where a lot of rhyming slang originates. It's not exactly *Loaded.*)

Harry Hill the pill
(There is a medical link as the surreal comedian born Matthew Hall practised as a doctor before turning to stand-up.)

Harry Lauder prison warder
(After the Scottish music-hall entertainer (1870–1950).)

Harry Lime time
(Harry Lime was the enigmatic central character in Graham Greene's 1950 novel *The Third Man*. In the film version Lime was played by Orson Welles who once famously summed up Switzerland's contribution to civilisation as the cuckoo clock, although it is extremely unlikely that this had any bearing on the choice of rhyme.)

Harry Randall handle
(An early twentieth-century rhyme, from the English music-hall comedian and celebrated pantomime dame (1860–1932).)

Harry Tate late, plate, state (mess)
(After the music-hall comedian (1872–1940) popular in the first part of the twentieth century.)

Harry Wragg fag (cigarette)
(English jockey (1902-85), nicknamed 'the Head Waiter' for his patient riding in a finish.)

Harvey Nichols pickles
(In honour of the upmarket department store founded in 1813 by Benjamin Harvey as a linen shop in London's Knightsbridge.)

Has beens greens (vegetables)

Hat and coat boat

Hat and feather weather

Hat and scarf bath

Hattie Jacques the shakes
(Comedy actress (1922–80) best known for playing Eric Sykes's sister in his long-running TV series and for appearing in fourteen *Carry On* films, notably as a formidable matron who would have given any patient the shakes.)

Heap of coke bloke
(From the days when London homes had coal fires, sometimes shortened to 'heapy'.)

Heart of oak broke (penniless)
(The lyrics for the rousing naval song 'Heart Of Oak' were written by David Garrick in the eighteenth century and the phrase has since become synonymous with courage. The idea behind the rhyme could be that you need plenty of courage if you've got no money.)

Heaven and hell smell

Heavenly bliss kiss

Hedge and ditch pitch

Henry Fonda Honda
(The US actor (1905–82) gave his name to the Honda 90

motorbike on which many aspiring taxi drivers toured the streets of London learning 'The Knowledge', their mental A-Z of the capital.)

Henry Halls balls (testicles)
(After the British bandleader (1898–1989), a popular radio personality whose 1932 recording of 'Teddy Bears' Picnic' sold over a million copies.)

Herbie Hides strides (trousers)
(British boxer Herbie Hide was twice WBO heavyweight champion in the 1990s. 'Strides' has been a colloquialism for 'trousers' since the start of the twentieth century, probably because trousers are clothes in which you stride.)

Here and there chair

Herring and kipper stripper

Hey diddle diddle fiddle
(Inspired by the eighteenth-century nursery rhyme and the increasing use of the word 'diddle' to mean 'cheat'.)

Hide and seek cheek (nerve)

Highland fling ring, king (in playing cards)

Hillman Hunter punter
(Named after the saloon car manufactured by Rootes from 1966 to 1979, the term was invented by second-hand car dealers but spread to include any type of customer perceived as a mug.)

Hit and miss kiss, piss
(Popular from the early 1960s, possibly inspired by the 'hit' or 'miss' cards held up by panellists on BBC television's *Juke Box Jury*, denoting whether or not they thought a record would reach the hit parade. A neat rhyme because both kissing and going for a pee can be hit and miss affairs, especially after a few drinks.)

Hobson's choice voice
(First recorded in 1937 and usually shortened to 'Hobson's', as in, 'That Peggy Mount had a Hobson's like a foghorn.' The phrase 'Hobson's choice' – meaning no choice at all – has been in use since 1660 and derives from Thomas Hobson (1545–1631), a Cambridge tradesman who used to hire out horses to students on condition that they always took the horse nearest the stable door.)

Hokey-cokey karaoke
(The hokey-cokey is a song and dance that originated in England during the early 1940s and quickly became popular among wartime Londoners. Karaoke – meaning 'empty orchestra' – started in Japan in the 1970s before developing into a worldwide phenomenon.)

Holy Ghost post (mail), toast

Home and away gay (homosexual)
(A rhyme that suggests batting for both sides. There is no obvious connection with the Australian soap of that title.)

Honey bees keys

Honey pot twat (vagina)

Hong Kong pong
(Although it means 'fragrant harbour' in Chinese, Hong Kong has not always lived up to its billing.)

Horn of Plenty twenty
(In Greek mythology the Horn of Plenty was the name given to a goat's horn filled with fruit and an abundance of other appetising foodstuffs.)

Horse and carriage garage

Horse and cart fart, tart
(Perhaps because the smell – from a fart rather than a tart – is similar to following a horse and cart. The expression is

usually shortened to 'orson', as in, 'Blimey, has somebody done an orson around here?')

Horse and trough cough
(Usually shortened to 'horse', whose similarity to 'hoarse' makes it suitable for a throaty rhyme.)

Horses and carts darts

Hot beef stop thief
(The word 'beef' has been used as a rhyme for 'thief' since at least the 1740s and in the nineteenth century 'hot beef' became the accepted Cockney cry aimed at a fleeing felon.)

Hot cross bun nun
(The cross on the bun is a symbol of the crucifixion (they are traditionally eaten on Good Friday) and the rhyme picks up on the religious significance, as in, 'Julie Andrews played a hot cross bun in *The Sound of Music*.')

Hot dinner winner
(Perhaps a reference to what a mug punter might finally be able to afford after backing a winner.)

Hot potato waiter
(A rhyme aided by the Cockney pronunciation 'potater'.)

House of Fraser razor
(House of Fraser is a chain of British department stores founded in Glasgow in 1849. When applied to cut-throat razors used by gangs, the term is generally reduced to 'howser'.)

House of Lords cords (corduroy trousers)

Housemaid's knee sea

Howards' Way gay (homosexual)
(The title of a BBC drama series (1985–90) set around a Hampshire boatyard and billed as the English answer to *Dallas* and *Dynasty*. Some of the acting was more wooden

than the boats while its occasionally camp approach undoubtedly contributed to the development of the rhyme.)

How's your father? lather (state)
(As in, 'Just because I was a few minutes late he was in a right how's your father.' In non-rhyming slang, 'how's your father' is a euphemism for 'sex'.)

Huckleberry Hound pound
(Created by Hanna-Barbera and voiced by Daws Butler, Huckleberry Hound had his own TV cartoon show from 1958, supported by Yogi Bear and Pixie and Dixie. A blue dog with a southern drawl and a penchant for singing 'Clementine', Huck lost out in the popularity stakes to Yogi but lives on in rhyming slang.)

Hugo Boss doss
(Based on the German clothing manufacturer (1885–1948).)

Hugs and kisses missus (wife)

Hundred to thirty dirty
(From horse-race betting odds, a shade over three to one.)

Hurricane lamp tramp

Hush Puppy yuppie
(Hush Puppies were a line of US-made pigskin shoes that arrived in Britain in 1961 with a sad-eyed basset hound as their trademark. Marketed primarily as sophisticated leisure shoes for the middle-aged, they enjoyed a sudden renaissance in the 1990s when affluent young urban professionals (yuppies) adopted them.)

Parlez-vous Cockney?

I went down the cab rank to sausage a goose's cos I'm short of bread until I get me greengages but the place was doublet and hosed. I was well Tom and Dick.

(I went down the bank to cash a cheque cos I'm short of money until I get me wages but the place was closed. I was well sick.)

I

I suppose nose
(First recorded in the 1850s, as in, 'What's that hanging from his I suppose?')

Ian Beale meal
(From the café that the character owned in *EastEnders*.)

Ian Rush brush
(At one stage in his career the prolific Liverpool goalscorer appeared to be wearing a brush on his top lip until he shaved it off.)

Ian Wright fright
(Similar to the apprehension experienced by opposing goal-keepers as the former Arsenal and England striker bore down on them... and by viewers when he later landed his own TV show.)

Ilie Nastase khazi (toilet)
(After the temperamental Romanian tennis player who brought the language of the gutter to Wimbledon in the 1970s.)

In and out gout

In the mood food

Incredible Hulk sulk
(Created by Stan Lee and Jack Kirby for *Marvel Comics* in 1962, Dr Bruce Banner is a scientist who, whenever he gets really angry, is transformed into a less than jolly green giant called the Incredible Hulk. The rhyme was inspired by the 1970s TV series and suggests that all around needed to be wary as soon as Banner went into even so much as a sulk.)

Inky blue flu
(Dating from the 1970s, this is possibly in recognition of the fact that anyone suffering from the flu is feeling decidedly blue.)

Inky smudge judge

Irish jig wig
(First used in the 1970s and generally shortened to 'Irish'.)

Irish stew true

Iron girder murder

Iron hoof poof
(First recorded in the 1930s and soon reduced to 'iron'. So it is not without irony that, besides being called 'the Hammers', West Ham United, the archetypal Cockney football club, are also nicknamed 'the Irons' – after their old name of Thames Ironworks.)

Iron Mike bike
(Based on the nickname of former world heavyweight boxing champion Mike Tyson.)

Iron tank bank

Isle of Man pan
(As in the London taxi driver's lament of, 'I dunno, the country's going right down the Isle of Man.')

Isle of Wight right

Itchy teeth beef

Ivory pearl girl
(As in, 'Diamonds are an ivory's best friend.')

J

J. Arthur Rank wank
(J. Arthur Rank (1888–1972) was the founder of the Rank Organisation, whose films always started with a man banging a gong. So the slang meaning may be symbolic as well as rhyming.)

J. Carroll Naish slash (urinate)
(From the American actor (1900–73) who played Charlie Chan in the 1950s TV series, as in, 'Hold me pint, I'm just going for a J. Carroll.')

J. K. Rowling bowling
(Harry Potter's creator is magically transformed into a rhyme for ten-pin bowling, as in, 'Are you going J. K. Rowling on Thursday?')

J. R. Ewing viewing (house)
(Estate agents' already battered reputations were dealt a further blow in the 1980s when they were likened to the scheming, murdering, philandering, lying, two-faced oil baron from *Dallas*. Or perhaps it was J. R. who should have been insulted by the comparison.)

Jabba the Hutt shut
(In honour of the obese, slug-like creature from *Star Wars*.)

Jack and Dandy handy

Jack and Danny fanny (vagina)
(From father and son characters in the 1980 horror film *The Shining*, based on Stephen King's novel.)

Jack and Jill hill, pill (contraceptive)
(Inspired by the traditional nursery rhyme, 'hill' is an obvious choice, but why the contraceptive pill? Perhaps Jill needed it because she went for a tumble afterwards.)

Jack Benny penny
(Violin-playing US comedian Jack Benny (1894–1974) built much of his stage act around his supposed penny-pinching. Other comics played up to it, Bob Hope once joking: 'They asked Jack Benny if he would do something for the Actors' Orphanage, so he shot both his parents and moved in.')

Jack Dee cup of tea
(The morose English comic looks as if he needs a cuppa to cheer him up.)

Jack Flash hash (cannabis)
(Almost certainly from the 1968 Rolling Stones' song 'Jumping Jack Flash'. The previous year band member Brian Jones had been arrested for possession of cannabis and both Mick Jagger and Keith Richards had been tried for possessing drugs.)

Jack in the box pox

Jack Jones on your own
(This rhyme originated during the First World War, as in, 'Now his hugs and kisses has left him, he's all on his Jack Jones.')

Jack Ketch stretch
(Jack Ketch was an English executioner of the seventeenth century, whose attention was therefore even less welcome to a convicted felon than a prison sentence or 'stretch'.)

Jack of Spades shades (sunglasses)

Jack Palance dance
(A US actor (1919–2006) of Ukrainian extraction who specialised in rugged roles rather than dance extravaganzas.)

Jack Sprat brat, fat
(Named after the world's most incompatible eaters – 'Jack Sprat could eat no fat, his wife could eat no lean.' Similarly when referring to a badly behaved child, the rhyme was first used to denote one who kicked up a fuss at mealtimes.)

Jack Straw draw (cannabis)
(In 1998 the then Home Secretary's son William was cautioned by police for selling cannabis to an undercover newspaper reporter.)

Jack tar bar
(A 'jack tar' is an old name for a sailor – derived from the tar with which sailors used to waterproof their trousers in the eighteenth century – and the rhyme owes much to the naval tradition which dictates that as soon as a ship arrives in port, the crew head for the nearest bar.)

Jack the Lad bad
(The original Jack the Lad was an eighteenth-century thief called Jack Sheppard but since the 1950s the phrase has been synonymous with any cocky young man who sails close to the wind and is generally up to no good.)

Jack the Ripper kipper
(The way in which a herring is sliced open is eerily reminiscent of the manner in which the 1888 Whitechapel serial killer slit open his victims.)

Jack the Rippers slippers

Jackanory story
(In rhyming slang 'jackanory' refers to a tall story (basically a lie) rather than the sort of tale read by Bernard Cribbins and co. on the BBC children's series *Jackanory* (1965–96).)

Jacket and vest West (End of London)
(As in, 'He must have something up his sleeve because he's going up the jacket this afternoon.')

Jackie Chan plan
(After the Chinese martial arts actor.)

Jackson Pollocks bollocks
(Not only rhyming slang, but also a critical appraisal of the work of the US abstract artist (1912–56).)

Jacob's Crackers knackers (testicles)
(From the cracker company that started life as W. & R. Jacob, a small biscuit bakery in Waterford, Ireland, in 1881.)

Jagger's lips chips
(The Rolling Stones frontman has been described as the only person on the planet with child-bearing lips. His most prominent features have been compared to many things over the years – notably wet-weather tyres – but rhyming slang offers a fresh perspective. Presumably the chips in question are the big fat ones.)

Jackie Brambles shambles
(An unkind dig at the TV presenter and former Radio 1 DJ.)

Jam roll parole, the dole

Jam tart heart

Jamaica rum thumb

James Blunt cunt
(The likes of Gareth Hunt have been well and truly usurped by the trill-voiced warbler who seems to have divided public opinion more than anything since Marmite.)

James Dean keen
(US actor (1931–55) whose premature death in a car crash proved a shrewd career move.)

James Hunt front (nerve)
(From the courageous and outspoken British racing driver (1947–93), as in, 'You ain't 'alf got some James Hunt!')

Jamjar car
(Originating in the 1930s, the term has achieved such widespread acceptance that the UK's biggest online new car dealer is called jamjar.com.)

Jammie dodger roger (fuck)
(In this case the 'jammie' in the biscuit may imply 'lucky'.)

Jane Fonda wander
(Possibly because after doing the American actress's fitness workouts you could walk for miles.)

Jane Shore whore
(Of all the royal mistresses past and present, it seems strange that Cockney rhymers should alight on the little-known Jane Shore, mistress of Edward IV in the fifteenth century.)

Janet Street-Porter quarter (of hashish)
(After the toothy TV 'yoof' programme pioneer and newspaper editor.)

Jarvis Cocker off his rocker
(A rhyme from the 1996 Brit Awards when the Pulp frontman gave the distinct impression of being off his rocker when he ran on stage and pointed his bum at Michael Jackson.)

Jasper Carrott parrot
(The Brummie comedian's real name of Bob Davis would only rhyme with a parrot if the bird's name was Mavis.)

Jay Kay takeaway
(A modern rhyme in honour of the Jamiroquai singer noted for his love of fast cars and exotic headgear.)

Jean Michel Jarre bar
(The first two-thirds of the French composer's name are also used to refer to a 'jar' (a pint glass) of beer. So you could order a Jean Michel while standing at the Jean Michel.)

Jeff Beck cheque
(A 1970s rhyme based on the influential English rock guitarist, formerly with The Yardbirds.)

Jeffrey Dahmer charmer
(A rhyme laden with irony to describe the cannibalistic US serial killer (1960–94) who was anything but a charmer.)

Jekyll and Hydes strides (trousers)
(From Robert Louis Stevenson's character with the split personality, usually shortened in rhyming slang to 'jekylls'.)

Jellied eel deal
(Thus Noel Edmonds presents the TV game show *Jellied Eel or No Jellied Eel?*.)

Jellied eels wheels (transport)
(As in, 'How are you getting home? Have you got jellied eels?')

Jelly bone phone

Jelly tot spot

Jenny Lind wind
(After the Swedish soprano (1820–87) who at some time in her career must have been backed by the wind section of the orchestra.)

Jeremy Beadle needle
(The British TV prankster (1948–2008) occasionally used to needle people with his practical jokes but most took them in good part.)

Jeremy Kyles piles
(Possibly chosen because the British talk show host is just as much a pain in the backside as haemorrhoids.)

Jerry Springer minger
(A 'minger' is modern slang for a young woman who fell out of the ugly tree at birth and hit every branch on the way

down. Mingers seem strangely drawn to appearing on confrontational talk shows such as those presented by Jerry Springer.)

Jet fighter all nighter

Jet lag fag (cigarette)

Jim Fenner tenner
(Named after the bad guy among all the *Bad Girls* in the ITV drama series (1999–2006) set in a women's prison.)

Jimi Hendrix appendix
(From the US rock guitarist (1942–70).)

Jimmy Choos shoes
(After the London-based fashion designer best known for his hand-crafted women's shoes.)

Jimmy Cliff whiff
(Based on the Jamaican reggae singer who enjoyed UK chart success in the late 1960s and early 1970s.)

Jimmy Connors honours
(Not relating to the honours the American won at tennis, but usually referring to an action like opening a bottle of champagne, as in, 'Will you do the Jimmy Connors, mate?')

Jimmy Greaves thieves
(As the outstanding goal poacher of his generation, footballer Jimmy Greaves stole countless points for Chelsea, Spurs and West Ham, scoring over 350 goals between 1957 and 1971.)

Jimmy Hill chill
(After the veteran footballer and broadcaster, as in, 'There's a bit of a Jimmy Hill in the air today.')

Jimmy Logie bogey
('Snot much fun for the Arsenal footballer (1919–84) being rhymed with nasal mucus.)

Jimmy Nail jail
(Before finding fame as a brickie in the 1980s TV series *Auf Wiedersehen, Pet,* Geordie actor/singer Jimmy Nail (real name James Bradford) served six months in Manchester's Strangeways Prison for GBH.)

Jimmy Page bird cage
(After the Led Zeppelin guitarist, as in, 'Have you seen all the poo on the bottom of the Jimmy Page?')

Jimmy Riddle piddle
(First recorded in the 1930s and has fought off stiff competition from bandleader Nelson (see **Nelson Riddle**) to become a universal byword for bladder-emptying. Sometimes shortened to just 'Jimmy', as in, 'Get 'em in while I go for a quick Jimmy.')

Jimmy Savile gravel, travel
(The 'travel' rhyme comes from the colourful DJ's long-running radio show *Savile's Travels,* but 'gravel' makes for an unusual pairing. After all, how many people's dream request to *Jim'll Fix It* would be for a new gravel path?)

Jimmy Shand banned
(Scottish accordionist and bandleader (1908–2000) who always appeared refreshed and relaxed when appearing on BBC Hogmanay programmes. This may account for why someone banned for drink-driving is said to have been 'Jimmy Shand'.)

Jimmy Young tongue
(The former singer and DJ used his tongue to good effect in a broadcasting career spanning 35 years even though he often seemed out of step with his younger colleagues on Radio 1 in the early 1970s. While they were playing Led Zeppelin or the Stones, JY was telling his listeners how to make an almond cake.)

Joan of Arc lark
(The name of the saint and French heroine (c.1412–31) is

mainly evoked in a sense of exasperation, as in, 'Blow this for a Joan of Arc!')

Joanna piano
(First recorded in 1846 and still going strong, 'joanna' is very much a Cockney knees-up piano. It is doubtful, for example, whether Liberace or Rachmaninoff ever referred to their instruments as 'joannas'.)

Jockey's whip kip (sleep)

Jockeys' whips chips

Jodie Marsh harsh
(The Essex-born glamour model is no stranger to making harsh comments about rival Jordan, once describing the latter's nose as 'hooked like a witch's'. In fairness it was in retaliation after Jordan had likened Marsh's breasts to 'spaniel's ears'. Girls, girls!)

Jodrell Bank wank
(Jodrell Bank is the name of a Cheshire observatory established in 1945 that is home to a number of radio telescopes.)

Joe Baksi taxi
(A US heavyweight boxer (1922–77), Baksi's name was frequently used as rhyming slang in Irvine Welsh's book *Trainspotting*.)

Joe Blake steak

Joe O'Gorman foreman

Joe Strummer bummer
(Born John Mellor, Joe Strummer (1952–2002) used to bum around the streets of London as a busker before finding fame as singer with punk-rock band The Clash. His Cockney rhyme is surely the only instance when his name will be mentioned in the same breath as John Selwyn Gummer. (See **John Selwyn Gummer**.))

John Bull on the pull
(A symbol of British nationalism, John Bull was created by
Dr John Arbuthnot in 1712. And what pursuit more typifies
the average British male – at least the under-30s – than going
on the pull?)

John Cleese cheese
(The comedy actor's family name was actually Cheese until
his father changed it in 1915.)

John Major wager
(You definitely could have got long odds on the grey man of
British politics having a steamy affair with Edwina Currie.)

John O'Groats oats
(As in, 'Look at the smile on his face – you can tell he's been
getting his John O'Groats lately.')

John Selwyn Gummer bummer
(The hapless Conservative politician who seemed to have
more bad days at the office than most, notably when as
Minister of Agriculture in 1990, at the height of the BSE
scare, he tried to make his four-year-old daughter Cordelia
eat a burger in public to prove that British beef was safe. The
poor girl probably thought the entire stunt was 'a real John
Selwyn'.)

John Wayne train
(The US Western actor (1907–79) was more familiar with a
wagon train than the 8.25 from Dartford to Charing Cross.)

John West very best
(From the fish producer whose TV adverts proclaimed that
only the best was good enough for John West. So when you
hear a Cockney saying, 'Send my John West to your mother,'
he is sending his best wishes rather than a tin of tuna.)

Johnnie Walker talker
(The rhyme is based on the brand of whisky, dating from the
nineteenth century, the implication being that too much of

it loosens your tongue. However, the loquacious aspect has been given added impetus since the 1960s by the British radio disc jockey born Peter Dingley who adopted Johnnie Walker as his professional name.)

Johnny Cash slash (urinate)
(After the US country singer (1932–2003).)

Johnny Depp step
(As in, 'She was so Oliver Twist she tripped over the Johnny Depp.')

Johnny Horner corner
(Dating from the late nineteenth century, this has surprisingly proved more durable in rhyming slang than the nursery rhyme character Jack Horner. Since pubs were invariably situated on street corners, 'going round the Johnny' meant going for a pint.)

Johnny Vaughan porn
(The English TV presenter who made his name on Channel 4's *The Big Breakfast* from 1997 to 2001.)

Jolly joker poker

Jolly Roger lodger
(Taken from the popular term for a pirate's flag that was first coined in the early eighteenth century and emphasising the commonly held view that lodgers weren't to be trusted. 'Roger' is also a slang term for having sex, the rhyme implying that as soon as the man of the house's back was turned, the lodger would be merrily taking advantage of his wife.)

Jonathan Ross toss
(After the irreverent broadcaster and chat show host, as in, 'I really couldn't give a Jonathan Ross!')

Jude Law score
(From the British actor, as in, 'Arsenal played West Ham tonight. Does anybody know the Jude Law?')

Judge Dredd head
(The law enforcer who first featured in the sci-fi comic *2000 AD* in 1977.)

Judith Chalmers farmers (piles)
(A once-removed rhyme linking the seasoned broadcaster who travelled the world in pink on *Wish You Were Here?* with an attack of 'farmers' (Farmer Giles = piles). (See **Farmer Giles**.))

Julian Clary fairy
(An obvious rhyme for the camp comic whose controversial, sexually explicit joke about politician Norman Lamont at the live 1993 British Comedy Awards resulted in the first known instance of sympathy for a Chancellor of the Exchequer.)

Julius Caesar geezer
(The distinguished Roman statesman (100–44 BC) might not have been too impressed had Brutus and Cassius referred to him as a 'geezer'.)

Jurassic Park dark
(A rhyme borrowed from the title of the 1993 dinosaur movie directed by Steven Spielberg and based on a novel by Michael Crichton.)

Just as I feared beard
(This is taken from a limerick in *The Book of Nonsense* (1846) by Edward Lear (1812–88): 'There was an Old Man with a beard, Who said, "It is just as I feared!" – Two Owls and a Hen, four Larks and a Wren, Have all built their nests in my beard.')

Parlez-vous Cockney?

I love the William Tell of Bernhard Langers and tent pegs frying in the Isle of Man first thing in the gypsy's warning, and then washed down by a nice Jack Dee.

(I love the smell of bangers and eggs frying in the pan first thing in the morning, and then washed down by a nice cup of tea.)

K

KY jelly telly
(Possibly based on the premise that some television can lubricate the mind.)

Kangaroo pouch couch

Kat Slater catch ya later
(At first glance *EastEnders*' Kat Slater, played by Jessie Wallace, was more of a dog than Wellard. But deep down she was a tart with a heart who was struggling to come to terms with her troubled past. Following an unlikely romance with Dr Anthony Trueman, she embarked on a volatile relationship with her eventual husband, Alfie Moon. (See also **Alfie Moon**.))

Kate and Sidney steak and kidney
(A partial spoonerism dating from the early twentieth century.)

Kate Carney army
(After the long-forgotten music-hall entertainer (1869–1950) who appeared in the 1935 Royal Variety Performance and specialised in comic Cockney songs.)

Kate Moss toss
(The waif-like model famous for her party lifestyle and on-off relationship with Pete Doherty.)

Kathy Burke work
(Character actress whose decision – partly made by God – to eschew glamour roles means that she is never short of work. She is probably best known for playing the hideous Waynetta Slob in *Harry Enfield and Chums* in the 1990s.)

Keira Knightley slightly
(A rhyme deriving from the actress's slight build, which prompted that noted beauty Jade Goody to describe Knightley's breasts as 'like two aspirins on an ironing board'.)

Keith Cheggers preggers (pregnant)
(From the nickname of TV presenter Keith Chegwin (see **Cheggers Plays Pop**).)

Keith Moon loon
(Keith Moon (1947–78) was the wildman drummer of The Who, his erratic behaviour earning the nickname 'Moon the loon'. He took peculiar delight in trashing hotel rooms, throwing TV sets out of windows and once even drove his Rolls-Royce into a swimming pool.)

Ken Dodd wad
(When the Liverpudlian comedian was charged with tax evasion in 1989, it was revealed that he kept a sizeable wad of money – £336,000 to be precise – stashed in suitcases in his attic.)

Kermit the frog bog (toilet)
(As a frog, the star of *The Muppet Show* would be quite at home in a bog.)

Kerry Katona moaner
(To Cockneys, this rhyme stems from the whiny Merseyside voice of the Atomic Kitten singer-turned-Iceland food shopper.)

Kerry Packered knackered
(From the Australian media mogul (1937–2005) who led a controversial international cricket breakaway in 1977. The state of exhaustion is usually expressed as 'kerried'.)

Kettle and hob fob (watch)

Khyber Pass arse
(A narrow gully flanked on either side by mountain ranges, the dangerous border pass between Afghanistan and

Pakistan bears a physical as well as a rhyming resemblance to an arse. Its popularity in Cockney rhyming slang was cemented by the 1968 film *Carry On Up the Khyber.*)

Kick and prance dance

Kick start tart (woman)

Kidney punch lunch
(As in, 'Do you fancy popping down the Rose and Crown for a spot of kidney?')

King Canutes boots
(An early twentieth-century rhyme based on the Danish king of England (reign 1016–35) who would have got his footwear wet as he tried to hold back the tide.)

King dick thick (stupid)

King Lear queer (gay)
(Shakespeare's tragic king is mainly summoned to rhyme in theatrical circles. Thus a bunch of thespians might be deemed 'a bit King Lear'.)

King Lears cars
(As in, 'That Mike Tyson only went and bit off a lump of Evander Holyfield's King Lear!')

Kingdom come bum

Kings and queens baked beans
(So 'beans on toast' becomes 'kings on holy ghost'.)

Kipper and bloater photo

Kipper and plaice face
(Another rhyme exploiting the common insult 'fish face'.)

Kiss and cuddle muddle

Kisses and hugs drugs

Kitchen sink clink (jail), drink

Kitty litter bitter (beer)

Knobbly knees keys
(In the 1950s many Londoners spent their summer break at the numerous holiday camps that were dotted around the coast. While the prettiest girls took part in beauty contests, the male equivalent was the knobbly knees contest, a harmless bit of fun to determine who had the dodgiest-looking knees.)

Knock at the door four

Knocker and knob job
(Possibly inspired by the old practice of going from door to door in search of work.)

Konnie Huq fuck
(The *Blue Peter* presenter from 1997–2008 has a legion of male fans, including Tony Blair and Gordon Brown, although their admiration is purely professional.)

Kuala Lumpur jumper
(A rhyme based on the capital of Malaysia, but use it sparingly in case animal rights activists take offence at hearing you say you're wearing a kuala.)

Kula Shaker sandwich maker
(From the 1990s band fronted by Crispian Mills, son of actress Hayley.)

Kung fu fighter cigarette lighter

Kurt Cobain cocaine
(A bleak rhyme for the US rock star (1967–94) whose cocaine and heroin habit contributed to his early demise.)

Kylie Minogues brogues (shoes)
(After the Australian pop princess, as in, 'What a lovely pair of Kylies!')

L

La-di-da cigar
(First recorded in 1977, a clear reference to the perceived superior social standing of cigar smokers. Sometimes abbreviated to 'lardy', which is particularly appropriate for a fat cigar.)

Lady Godiva fiver
(According to legend, Lady Godiva, the wife of Leofric, Earl of Mercia, rode naked through the streets of Coventry in the eleventh century to persuade her husband to lower taxes. In rhyming slang, she represents a fiver. Thus a 'commodore' is £15, i.e. three times a 'lady'.)

Lady in silk milk

Lager and lime time

Lager lout kraut (German)
(A 1990s insult for the nation that brews arguably the best lager in the world.)

Lambeth Walk chalk
(Written by Douglas Furber and Noel Gay, 'The Lambeth Walk' was a song-and-dance number from the 1937 musical *Me and My Girl*. The 'chalk' in the rhyme is for snooker, billiards and pool cues.)

Lame duck fuck

Larry Grayson Mason
(From the camp comic (1923–95) whose catchphrase 'Shut that door' and unseen friend Everard helped propel him to national prominence in the 1970s. The origins of the rhyme may lie in the suspicion with which Masons and

homosexuals are treated in certain circles. Used as in, 'Do you reckon he's a Larry?')

Last card of the pack the sack
(A rhyme inspired by the expression 'getting your cards', meaning 'to get the sack'.)

Laugh and joke smoke (cigarette)
(A rhyme that was popular in the first half of the twentieth century when men and women would gather for a laugh and joke while enjoying a smoke.)

Laugh and titter bitter (beer)

Laurel and Hardy Bacardi
(After the comic giants of the 1930s. (See also **Stan and Ollie**.))

Left and right fight
(A neat rhyme conjuring up images of blows in a boxing match.)

Left in the lurch church
(A nineteenth-century phrase that must have been particularly poignant for any bride left waiting at the altar.)

Leg of beef thief

Lemon and lime crime

Lemon curd bird (girl), turd
(As with 'Richard the Third', the exact meaning should be evident from the context, although dumping either can be a painful experience.)

Lemon drop cop (police officer)

Lemon squeezer geezer

Lemon squeezy easy
(As in the familiar children's rhyme 'easy peasy lemon squeezy'.)

Lemon tart smart

Len Hutton button
(From the Yorkshire and England batsman (1916–90) who captained his country in the 1950s but is best remembered for his 13-hour innings of 364 against Australia at the Oval in 1938, which broke the record for the highest individual score in a Test match.)

Lenny the Lion iron (homosexual)
(A rhyme on a rhyme (see **Iron hoof**) and based on the rather camp puppet lion partnered by ventriloquist Terry Hall. With his catchphrase 'Don't embawass me', Lenny was such a popular feature of children's TV in the early 1960s that The Beatles were once guests on his show. And among the members of Lenny's thriving fan club was eight-year-old David Jones who went on to find fame as David Bowie.)

Leo Fender bender (homosexual)
(American Leo Fender (1909–91) was the founder of the trailblazing electric guitar manufacturing company. He was happily married to his first wife for 45 years.)

Les Dennis menace, tennis
(The entertainer surely owes his appearance in rhyming slang partly to Dennis the Menace, the mischievous boy who has graced the *Beano* comic since 1951.)

Leslie Ash slash (urinate)
(A 1990s rhyme from the time when the comedy actress was the object of male fantasies in the sitcom *Men Behaving Badly* – and before the unfortunate collagen lip implants that left her with the infamous 'trout pout'.)

Lester Piggott bigot
(Famously monosyllabic British jockey who rode over 5,000 winners, including nine Epsom Derbies, and served a jail sentence in 1987 for tax evasion.)

Life and death breath

Lilley and Skinner beginner
(After the British shoe manufacturers founded in 1835.)

Lillian Gish fish
(Hollywood actress (1893–1993) who began her career in 'the silents' and made her final film in 1987 at the age of 93.)

Lily the Pink drink
(The title of The Scaffold's 1968 number one, the chorus of which contains the line, 'We'll drink a drink a drink to Lily the Pink the Pink the Pink.' It was loosely based on a ribald folk song, 'The Ballad of Lydia Pinkham', the story of an American woman who in the nineteenth century concocted herbal and alcoholic tonics to relieve menstrual and menopausal pains. In The Scaffold's version, Lily's medicinal compound could cure everything from Johnny Hammer's t-t-terrible s-s-stammer to Mr Frears's sticky-out ears.)

Limehouse Cut gut (paunch)
(The oldest canal in London, the Limehouse Cut provides a short cut from the Thames at Limehouse Basin to the River Lee Navigation.)

Linda Lusardi cardy (cardigan)
(In her days as a Page Three model, she never had so much as a cardy to hide her assets.)

Linen draper newspaper
(Dating from the nineteenth century and usually shortened to 'linen'.)

Lion's lair chair
(This twentieth-century rhyme is based on the notion that the head of the house has his favourite chair and that it is unwise – dangerous even – for anyone else to attempt to sit in it.)

Lion's roar snore

Lionel Bart fart
(After the composer of musicals born Lionel Begleiter (1930–99), the Andrew Lloyd Webber of the early 1960s.

Unfortunately it all went wrong with his short-lived 1965 offering *Twang!!*, based on the story of Robin Hood, which critics found about as welcome as a fart in a phone box.)

Lionel Blair chair

Lionel Blairs flares (trousers)
(After the happy hoofer who carried off the seventies fashions with more style than most.)

Lionel Hampton hampton (penis)
(Another double rhyme (see **Hampton Wick**), this time after US jazz musician Lionel Hampton (1908–2002).)

Lionel Richie itchy
(From the US singer, as in, 'This new kuala makes my skin Lionel Richie.')

Lisa Tarbucks Starbucks
(An obvious rhyme between the actress daughter of comedian Jimmy Tarbuck and the US coffee-house chain which started out in Seattle in 1971 as a single store and now boasts more than 15,000 outlets worldwide.)

Little and large marge (margarine)
(This rhyming slang is not thought to be connected to the comedy double act of Syd Little and Eddie Large, whose BBC TV show ran from 1978 to 1991, although just as margarine was considered a poor substitute for butter most critics considered Little and Large to be a poor substitute for Morecambe and Wise.)

Little brown jug plug
(Derived from the 1869 song 'Little Brown Jug' by Joseph Winner that was popularised 70 years later by Glenn Miller. The 'plug' in question can be anything from a bath fitting to a tampon.)

Little Nell bell
(From the tragic character in Charles Dickens's *Old Curiosity*

Shop. The term is usually applied to a doorbell, as in, 'Who's that ringing on the Little Nell at this hour?')

Little Red Riding Hoods stolen goods
(From the Brothers Grimm fairytale and given added poignancy these days by the association of hoodies with crime.)

Little Tich itch
(Little Tich was the stage name of 4ft 6in music-hall comedian Harry Relph (1867–1928) whose most celebrated routine was his Big Boot Dance, for which he wore a pair of 28-inch boots.)

Live gig frig (female masturbation)

Liz Hurley early
(Glamorous British actress and model whose success in America makes her Basingstoke's most famous export.)

Loaf of bread dead, head
(While 'loaf of bread' was originally rhyming slang for both 'dead' and 'head', it is the second meaning, dating back to the late nineteenth century, which has survived. It is always shortened to 'loaf', as in the familiar expression 'use your loaf' (meaning 'be sensible'), which first appeared in print in 1938. Coleen McLoughlin could be said to have used her loaf when standing by Wayne Rooney whereas Paul McCartney must have been a few sandwiches short of a picnic when he married Heather Mills.)

Lollipop shop
(This can be used in the sense of 'to inform on' as well as to denote a retail outlet.)

London Bridge fridge
(A bridge has existed at or near the present site for nearly 2,000 years. The current London Bridge – at least the seventh – was opened in 1973.)

London fog dog
(When householders burned coal fires, dense fogs – or pea soupers or smogs as they became known – hung ominously over London for days at a time. The Great Smog of 1952 brought the capital to a standstill for four days and was responsible for over 4,000 deaths mainly from respiratory problems.)

London taxi jacksie (backside)

Long Acre baker
(A rhyme first recorded in the nineteenth century and named after the street near Covent Garden, even though the road has no links with baking.)

Looby Loos shoes
(After the doll in the 1950s children's TV series *Andy Pandy*, as in, 'Check out the new Loobies.')

Loop the loop soup
(It must have been a strange dream that came up with a rhyme based on a daring aerobatic manoeuvre performed over a bowl of cream of tomato.)

Lord and mastered plastered (drunk)

Lord Lovell shovel
(The rhyme has its origins among nineteenth-century sailors although nobody is sure which of the many Lord Lovells it actually concerns.)

Lord Mayor swear
(Perhaps because the Lord Mayor of London has to swear allegiance to the sovereign.)

Lord of the Manor tanner (sixpence)
(Introduced in 1551, the sixpence – nicknamed a 'tanner' and the equivalent of 2½p – continued in circulation until decimalisation in 1971, four years after the last coin was put on general issue. The rhyme dates back to the mid-nineteenth century and was generally shortened to 'lord'.)

Lord Sutch crotch (groin)
(Screaming Lord Sutch was the stage name of 1960s shock rock star David Sutch (1940–99) who, backed by his band The Savages, began shows by emerging from a coffin and dressed as Jack the Ripper. In 1963 he turned his attention to politics, standing at the Stratford-upon-Avon by-election as a representative of the National Teenage Party. Twenty years later he founded the Official Monster Raving Loony Party and in his flamboyant attire he livened up the British political scene, standing in a total of 40 by-elections. Despite his outward exuberance he suffered from depression and took his own life by hanging himself.)

Lords and peers ears

Lorna Doone spoon
(Inspired by the heroine of Exmoor from the 1869 novel *Lorna Doone* by R. D. Blackmore.)

Lose or win foreskin

Lost and found pound

Lou Reed speed (amphetamines)
(American singer/songwriter Lou Reed has written songs about drugs, not to mention S&M, oral sex and transvestism.)

Love and kisses missus

Lover's tiff syph (syphilis)
(A cleverly understated rhyme as to the likely outcome when one partner learns that the other has syphilis.)

Lucky charm arm

Lucky dip chip, kip (sleep)

Lucy Locket pocket
(From the nineteenth-century nursery rhyme: 'Lucy Locket lost her pocket, Kitty Fisher found it; Not a penny was there

in it, Only ribbon round it.' Lucy Locket was a London barmaid in the 1700s, and the 'pocket' in the rhyme apparently refers to her 'lover', although it was also a euphemism for the pouch in which prostitutes kept their money and which they used to tie to their thigh with a ribbon. Kitty Fisher was equally disreputable, being an aspiring actress and serial mistress.)

Lump of ice advice

Lump of lead head

Parlez-vous Cockney?

I'm in a right kiss and cuddle – the London fog's eaten me frying pan's Michael Winner, there's didn't oughta all over the Rory O'Moore in the Kermit, and the Jolly Roger's scarpered without paying his Burton.

(I'm in a right muddle – the dog's eaten me old man's dinner, there's water all over the floor in the bog, and the lodger's run off without paying his rent.)

M

Macaroni pony (£25)
(A 'macaroni' was an eighteenth-century English term for a dandy. The rhyme with 'pony' stems from the mocking song 'Yankee Doodle', a British jibe at US fashions at the time of the American War of Independence (1775–83). The song began: 'Yankee Doodle went to town, Riding on a pony; He stuck a feather in his hat, And called it macaroni.' So it has nothing to do with pasta. (See also **Yankee Doodles**.))

Mackerel and sprat prat

Mae West best, chest
(After the amply proportioned American actress (1893–1980) who specialised in sexual innuendo. Her chest was so admired by Allied soldiers during the Second World War that they called their yellow inflatable life jackets 'Mae Wests' because the shape reminded them of her generous bosom.)

Magistrate's court short (drink)
(Probably a warning as to where you are likely to end up if you drink too many shorts.)

Magnus Pyke dyke (lesbian)
(Dr Magnus Pyke (1908–92) was the fast-talking, arm-waving, eccentric scientist who co-presented the 1970s TV series *Don't Ask Me*. In fact he was more a human windmill than that other Dutch geographical feature, the dyke.)

Mahatma Gandhi brandy
(Named after the Indian nationalist leader and teetotaller (1869–1948).)

Major Loder whisky and soda
(Major Eustace Loder owned and bred the racehorse Pretty
Polly, winner of 22 of her 24 races between 1903 and 1906.
Her legend lives on in the form of the Pretty Polly Stakes run
annually at Newmarket. Major Loder may well have cele-
brated her success with a whisky and soda.)

Major Stevens evens (betting odds)
(A fictitious character to describe a situation when the odds
are one to one or fifty-fifty.)

Man alive five

Man and wife knife

Man on the moon spoon

Mandy Dingle single
(Played by Lisa Riley, Mandy Dingle was a larger-than-life
character from the ITV soap *Emmerdale*. She was the proud
owner of an unfeasibly large chest, which kept one side of
the Pennines in permanent shade. She was married first to
her cousin Butch and then to local vet Paddy Kirk but left
the village in 2001 and is currently believed to be single.)

Manfred Mann plan
(South African-born keyboard player whose band had a
string of hits in the 1960s, including 'Do Wah Diddy Diddy'
and 'Pretty Flamingo'. His real name was Manfred Lubowitz
but he took his stage moniker from American jazz drummer
Shelley Manne.)

Mangle and wringer singer
(A mangle and wringer was a common sight in British
households before the advent of washing machines in the
late 1950s.)

Manhole cover brother
(A partly anatomical expression to rhyme with the Cockney
'bruvver', as in Joe Brown's old backing band. So in Cockney

rhyming slang The Hollies' 1969 hit was titled 'He Ain't Heavy, He's My Manhole Cover'.)

Marble halls balls (testicles)
(Shortened to 'marbles', this nineteenth-century rhyme owes much to their shape. The game itself dates back to the days of ancient Egypt when it was played with pebbles or balls of clay. The mass manufacture of glass marbles began in 1890 but it was not until the 1950s that the Japanese introduced the familiar cat's eye marble, created by injecting coloured glass into a regular marble.)

Marble slabs crabs (pubic lice)

Marbles and conkers bonkers

Margate sands hands

Maria Monk spunk (semen)
(Maria Monk was the name of a Canadian nun who claimed to have been sexually abused in her Montreal convent and whose sensational revelations were published in the anonymously written 1836 tome, *Awful Disclosures of Maria Monk*. It has since been generally accepted that her story was false and that the episode was nothing more than anti-Catholic propaganda.)

Mariah Carey scary
(The singer's alleged demands make her scary enough, such as the insistence that her hotel suite be fitted with gold faucets and that she be given cute puppies to stroke before making a TV appearance. Carey herself protested recently: 'I've never done one diva-ish thing in my life. The actual definition of a diva is a woman who sings well.' Enough said.)

Marie Corelli telly
(An early rhyme for television taken from the pseudonym of the British romantic novelist Mary Mackay (1855–1924), the Barbara Cartland of her day.)

Marilyn Manson handsome
(From the outrageous American musician – real name Brian Warner – whose appearance redefines 'handsome'.)

Market stalls balls (testicles)

Marquis de Sade hard
(French aristocrat and writer (1740–1814) whose pleasure at inflicting pain on others gave rise to the term 'sadism' and probably made him think he was well hard.)

Mars and Venus penis

Mars bar scar
(Introduced in 1932, the Mars bar boasts such famous fans as explorer Sir Ranulph Fiennes, who claims to eat four at a time, Joan Collins, Paul Gascoigne and, of course, Marianne Faithfull. The phrase entered Cockney rhyming slang in the 1970s, chiefly to denote the sort of scar received in a gang fight.)

Marti Pellow yellow (snooker ball)
(After the Wet Wet Wet singer (real name Mark McLachlan).)

Martin Kemp hemp
(Former member of 1980s band Spandau Ballet who later turned his talents to starring in *EastEnders* and advertising sofas.)

Marty Wilde mild (beer)
(From Marty Wilde (real name Reg Smith) who was a pioneering British rock 'n' roll singer of the late 1950s and enjoyed renewed interest 30 years later as Kim's dad.)

Mary Ellens melons (big breasts)
(Perhaps originating from the old music-hall song 'I'm Shy, Mary Ellen, I'm Shy', written by George A. Stevens.)

Maud and Ruth truth

Max Factor actor
(A rhyme taken from the international cosmetics firm founded in 1909 by a Russian make-up artist based in the US.)

Max Walls balls (testicles)
(Usually abbreviated to 'Maxies', this rhyme is named after the English comedian (1908–90) best known for his eccentrically attired character Professor Wallofski.)

Megadeth bad breath
(After the US heavy metal band, with the suggestion that death from halitosis would be a particularly horrible way to go.)

Melvyn Bragg shag
(The doyen of the arts might have hoped for a worthier memorial than an act of rough copulation.)

Merchant banker wanker
(A 1980s jibe from a time when flash city yuppies antagonised the working man by earning obscene amounts of money. Although their talents appeared minimal to the outsider, at least the rhyme implies that their left hand usually knew what their right hand was doing.)

Merry-go-round pound
(Suggesting the circulation of currency.)

Merry old soul coal
(From the eighteenth-century nursery rhyme 'Old King Cole', who was a merry old soul.)

Meryl Streep cheap
(After the Oscar-winning US actress.)

Mexican wave shave
(The ultimate sign of spectator boredom at a sporting event first manifested itself at the 1986 Mexico World Cup.)

Michael Caine pain, stain
(The actor's London roots – in his youth he worked as a

porter at Smithfield meat market – make him a natural for Cockney rhyming slang even though he has had barely a stain on his character in a career spanning more than forty years.)

Michael Miles piles
(The New Zealand-born 'Quiz Inquisitor' (1919–71) who hosted the popular ITV game show *Take Your Pick* from 1955 to 1968. His association with haemorrhoids is as tenuous as rumours that he was an alcoholic. In fact he was an epileptic who was so ashamed of his condition that he used to lock himself in his dressing room, preferring to be thought drunk.)

Michael Schumachers knackers (testicles)
(Particularly apt because *Schumacher* is German for 'cobbler'.)

Michael Winner dinner
(A simple rhyme for the food critic and *bon viveur*.)

Mickey Duff rough
(The British boxing promoter's battered face is testament to his own pugilistic past.)

Mickey Monk drunk

Mickey Mouse house

Mickey Mouser Scouser
(Since his debut in 1928, the Walt Disney rodent's name has come to be a colloquialism for 'substandard' or 'amateurish'. Consequently Cockney football fans love to taunt their Liverpool counterparts as being precisely that.)

Mickie Most toast
(After the record producer (1938–2003) who brought the world Suzi Quatro and was a regular judge on the 1970s TV talent show *New Faces*.)

Mile End friend
(From the area of East London that gets its name because it is one mile east of the boundary of the City of London.)

Milky Way gay (homosexual)

Millennium Dome comb
(An ironic rhyme since a bald dome has no need of a comb.)

Milton Keynes jeans
(A late twentieth-century rhyme following on from the founding of the Buckinghamshire new town in 1967. Whereas once it was a small village it is now a thriving city with plenty of shops in which to buy a new pair of Miltons.)

Mince pies eyes
(First recorded in 1857 and generally shortened to 'minces', as in, to paraphrase The Eagles, 'You can't hide those lyin' minces.')

Minnie Driver fiver
(After the English actress and singer.)

Miss Fitch bitch
(Nobody knows who Miss Fitch was or what she had done to earn such condemnation in the early twentieth century.)

Mr Shifter shirtlifter (homosexual)
(Mr Shifter was a piano removal character in a 1970s TV advert for PG Tips tea starring the famous Brooke Bond chimps. There is no suggestion that the chimp in question was the slightest bit 'fromage frais'.)

Moan and wail jail

Moby Dick sick
(From the fearsome great white whale in the 1851 novel *Moby Dick* by Herman Melville.)

Mods and rockers knockers (breasts)
(In the mid-1960s, British seaside towns were turned into

battlegrounds on Bank Holidays as gangs of parka-wearing, scooter-riding mods clashed with leather-jacketed, motorbike-riding rockers. Seen as epitomising a decline in moral standards among the young, both groups had their knockers – but not in the Pamela Anderson sense.)

Mona Lisa pizza
(One Italian work of art representing another even though Leonardo Da Vinci probably never envisaged *La Gioconda* with an anchovy topping.)

Monkey spanker wanker
(From the modern slang 'spank the monkey' meaning 'to masturbate'. The exact derivation of monkey spanking is unclear although some sources suggest that 'monkey' is American slang for male genitals.)

Monkey's tail nail

Monks' habits rabbits
(This rhyme stems from the contrasting morals of monks and rabbits.)

Monty's army barmy
(The troops in question were those commanded by General Montgomery in the Second World War as opposed to the 'Barmy Army' of England cricket supporters paying homage to spinner and cult hero Monty Panesar.)

Moonlight flits tits

More or less dress
(This is supposedly based on how much you can see in terms of cleavage or thigh as dictated by changing fashion trends.)

Morecambe and Wise flies
(Eric Morecambe (1926–84) and Ernie Wise (1925–99) were a much-loved comedy double act for 43 years until Eric's death, attracting the biggest names in show business – and Des O'Connor – to appear on their TV series in the 1970s.)

Moriarty party
(It seems unlikely that the Moriarty in question is either Sherlock Holmes's arch enemy, Professor Moriarty, or Spike Milligan's Count Jim Moriarty from *The Goon Show*. Therefore the origins of the rhyme remain a mystery.)

Mork and Mindy windy
(A 1978 spinoff from *Happy Days, Mork and Mindy* made a star of Robin Williams as the alien Mork from the planet Ork.)

Morris Minor shiner (black eye), vagina
(The original Morris Minor was produced from 1928 to 1933 but the more familiar model ran from 1948 to 1971, during which time more than 1.6 million were sold.)

Mortar and trowel towel

Mother Goose loose
(The nursery rhyme character was first recorded in France in the seventeenth century and according to legend is based on Bertha *pied d'oie* (Goose-foot Bertha), wife of King Robert II who ruled France from 996 to 1031.)

Mother Hubbard cupboard
(From the sad tale – first published in 1805 – of Old Mother Hubbard who went to the cupboard to fetch her poor dog a bone, only to find that the shelves were bare. This was of course long before Asda introduced late-night shopping.)

Mother Kelly jelly
(From the much-loved music hall song 'On Mother Kelly's Doorstep', written by George A. Stevens in 1925.)

Mother-in-law saw
(No doubt stemming from the fact that one has a sharp tongue and the other has sharp teeth.)

Mother of pearl girl

Mother's pride bride
(A soppy sentimental rhyme unless the composer was thinking of the sliced bread that was first sold in the UK in 1936.)

Mountain bike dyke (lesbian)

Mountain passes glasses

Mountains of Mourne horn (erection)
(Probably from the way they rise majestically above the Northern Ireland landscape.)

Mrs Moore floor
(From the character in the 1926 Harry Castling and James Walsh comic song 'Don't Have Any More, Mrs Moore'. The rhyme is frequently shortened to 'the Mrs', as in 'Oi, don't tread your muddy boots all over the Mrs!')

Mrs Mopp shop
(A 1940s expression taken from the charlady character in the radio comedy *ITMA* starring Tommy Handley. Standing for 'It's That Man Again' (a reference to Hitler), *ITMA* ran from 1939 to 1949 and its many catchphrases – including Mrs Mopp's 'Can I do you now, sir?' – helped maintain British morale during the war.)

Muddy trench the bloody French
(A rhyme dug out in the trenches of the First World War.)

Mum and Dad mad

Murray Mint skint
(A line of confectionery that became part of popular culture in the late 1950s thanks to a series of amusing TV commercials – when adverts were still a novelty – for the 'too good to hurry mint'. And in those days sweets were still cheap enough not to leave you skint.)

Murray Walker talker
(If ever a rhyme suited a celebrity, it is to label the veteran motor racing commentator a 'talker'. Motormouth Murray

was never at a loss for words, even if they didn't always come out in the right order. On his own admission, he sometimes got carried away, his frenetic style being described by Clive James as sounding 'like a man whose trousers are on fire'.)

Mustard and cress dress

Muswell Hill bill
(From the district of north London, as in, 'Oi, cheese grater, can I have the Muswell?')

Mutt and Jeff deaf
(Mutt and Jeff were two dim-witted comic strip characters – the former tall, the latter short – created by Bud Fisher in 1907 for the *San Francisco Chronicle*. They entered rhyming slang around the 1930s, but are sometimes abbreviated to 'mutton', as in, 'He must be a bit mutton not to have heard that box of toys last night.')

Mutter and stutter butter

Myleene Klass ass
(The former member of Hear'Say is probably relieved to learn that she is paired with a shapely bottom rather than a donkey, as in the builders' shout of approval: 'Oi, nice Myleene!')

Myrna Loy saveloy
(Actress Myrna Loy (1905–93) may have been voted 'Queen of Hollywood' in 1938 but in the world of Cockney rhymesters her finest achievement is giving her name to a spicy sausage.)

Mystic Megs legs
(After the tabloid astrologer from Accrington (real name Margaret Anne Lake) who made her eerie presence felt on the first televised National Lottery draws in 1994.)

N

Nanny goat coat, throat
(Usually abbreviated to 'nanny', as in, 'I've got a frog in my nanny.')

Nat King Cole the dole
(From the unforgettable African-American singer (1919–65), as in, 'Are you gonna spend your entire life on the Nat King Cole?')

Natasha Kaplinsky kinky
(A modern rhyme after the glamorous TV newsreader waspishly nicknamed 'Spangles' by a female journalist.)

National Front cunt

Naughton and Gold cold
(Along with Flanagan and Allen and Nervo and Knox (see **Nervo and Knox**), Charlie Naughton (1887–1976) and Jimmy Gold (1886–1967) were one of the three double acts that made up the comedy troupe known as the Crazy Gang. Great favourites of the royal family, the Crazy Gang's zany antics reigned supreme on the British stage from the 1930s to the 1960s.)

Needle and pin gin, thin
(Both meanings were first recorded in the 1930s, the second being particularly suitable because even the average supermodel isn't quite as thin as a needle or pin.)

Needle and thread bread

Needles and pins twins
(As in, 'Congratulations, you've got needles!' Giving birth to

twins should not be confused with the less painful and non-life-changing experience of pins and needles.)

Nell Gwynn gin
(Charles II's mistress (1650–87) was famed for selling oranges, which just happen to go very nicely with gin.)

Nellie Dean queen (homosexual)
(After the central figure in the music-hall song written by Harry Armstrong in 1905. Hence the slang word 'nellie' for an effeminate man.)

Nellie Deans greens

Nellie Duff puff (life)
(This rhyme is the origin of the phrase 'not on your nellie', first heard in the 1940s and meaning 'not on your life', since 'puff' is slang for 'life'. *Not On Your Nellie* was also the title of a 1970s sitcom starring the redoubtable Hylda Baker.)

Nelson Eddys readies (cash)
(From American singer Nelson Eddy (1901–67) who spent most of his career crooning on horseback to Jeanette MacDonald but in doing so proved successful enough to ensure that he was never short of readies.)

Nelson Mandela Stella (Artois)
(Whether the South African statesman has ever sunk a pint of Stella is open to debate.)

Nelson Riddle piddle
(A wee honour for the US composer and orchestra leader (1921–85).)

Nervo and Knox goggle box (TV)
(Although mainly at home on the stage, Crazy Gang duo Jimmy Nervo (1890–1975) and Teddy Knox (1896–1974) made occasional appearances on black and white TV in the days when it was still called the 'goggle box' (see also **Naughton and Gold**).)

Nervous wreck cheque
(A rhyme drawing on the emotions felt while waiting for a large payment to arrive in the post.)

New Delhi belly
(This term is derived from the rush of diarrhoea known as 'Delhi belly' that sometimes results from eating poorly prepared Indian food on the sub-continent.)

Newgate Gaol tale
(The tale in question is the type of hard-luck yarn that might be spun by a prisoner. Newgate was the notorious jail that operated for over 700 years on the site of what is now the Old Bailey. It first opened in 1188 and after being rebuilt many times, closed in 1902 and was finally demolished two years later. Its famous inmates included author Daniel Defoe, playwright Ben Jonson and anti-Catholic conspirator Titus Oates.)

Newington Butts guts
(After a road in Southwark where archery was once practised, with mounds of earth serving as targets. These practice fields were known as 'butts'. In rhyming slang it refers chiefly to stomach ache, as in, 'I've got a real Michael Caine in my Newingtons.')

Newton and Ridley tiddly (drunk)
(The inevitable outcome of drinking too much beer in *Coronation Street*'s Rover's Return, purveyor of fine ales from the fictitious Newton and Ridley brewery since at least 1960.)

Niagara Falls balls (testicles)
(In use since the 1950s and usually abbreviated to 'Niagaras'.)

Nice one, Cyril squirrel
(From a catchphrase that started life in a 1970s TV commercial for Wonderloaf and spread to the football terraces where Spurs fans sang it in praise of their left-back Cyril Knowles (1944–91).)

Nicole Richie bitchy
(Without wishing to sound bitchy, the daughter of Lionel appears to be famous solely for her turbulent celebrity lifestyle.)

Nigel Mansell cancel
(After the 1992 Formula One world champion who was also twice voted BBC Sports Personality… despite not appearing to have one.)

Night and day grey

Night Boat to Cairo giro
('Night Boat To Cairo' was the title of a track on the 1979 debut album by London 'Nutty Boys' Madness, subsequently reissued in 1993 as a single. 'Giro' is a slang term for 'the dole', arising from the name of the cheque given to those on social security.)

Niki Lauda powder (cocaine)
(After the Austrian Formula One driver badly hurt in a crash at the 1976 German Grand Prix.)

Nits and lice price
(The 'price' here refers to the betting odds offered by a bookmaker, as in, 'What's the nits on Saucy Sue in the 3.45 at Sandown?')

No surrenders suspenders

Noah's Ark lark, nark (informant), park

Nobby Stiles piles
(Fittingly trimmed to 'Nobbies' in honour of the combative Manchester United and England footballer whose toothless jig after the 1966 World Cup final earned him the status of national treasure.)

Noddy Holders shoulders
(If Charlotte Church has the voice of an angel, Noddy

Holder, the singer with 1970s band Slade, had the voice of a pneumatic drill.)

Noel Gallagher week in Malaga
(Finding the outspoken Oasis frontman on the next sunbed to you in Spain might not exactly be conducive to a quiet holiday, especially if he's got brother Liam in tow.)

Nook and cranny fanny (vagina)

North and south mouth
(Dating back to the mid-nineteenth century, this phrase was still commonplace 100 years later, as illustrated by Cockney singer Tommy Steele's 1960 recording 'What a Mouth', which contained the lines: 'What a mouth, what a mouth, what a north and south, Blimey what a mouth he's got!')

Nose and chin win
(The abbreviated version 'nose' may be the basis of the expression 'on the nose', a horse-racing term describing a bet laid for a win only rather than each way.)

Nuclear sub pub

Nuremberg Trials piles
(In the German city of Nuremberg between 1945 and 1946, 24 leading Nazis were tried for war crimes and crimes against humanity in what became known as the Nuremberg Trials.)

Nursery rhymes *The Times*
(A whimsical rhyme linking a children's pursuit with arguably Britain's most grown-up newspaper.)

Nutcrackers knackers (testicles)
(Presumably inspired by 'nuts' being slang for 'testicles'.)

Parlez-vous Cockney?

The trouble and strife's gone Mrs Mopping for an Auntie Ella but if we do get a David Gower she'd be better off spending her Nelson Eddies on a new nanny.

(The wife's gone shopping for an umbrella but if we do get a shower she'd be better off spending her readies on a new coat.)

O

Oats and barley charlie (cocaine)
(This is one of the few instances in rhyming slang where the shortened form consists of the last word – 'barley', probably to avoid any confusion with 'getting your oats'.)

Obi-Wan Kenobi mobi (mobile phone)
(After the Jedi Master from *Star Wars*.)

Ocean liner shiner (black eye)

Ocean wave shave

Oedipus Rex sex
(From the character in Greek mythology who killed his father, married his mother, committed incest with her and later had a complex about the whole thing.)

Office worker shirker
(A rhyme devised by manual labourers to convey the impression that people employed in an office just sit behind their desks all day and don't know the meaning of hard work.)

Ogden Nash slash (urinate)
(After the US poet (1902–71) renowned for his humorous verse.)

Ogle and leer gonorrhoea

Oi Jimmy Knacker tobacco
(Oi Jimmy Knacker was a children's street game similar to leapfrog that was popular in London in the 1920s. The rhyme works because of the Cockney pronunciation 'tabakker'.)

Oil leak Sikh

Oil slick spick (Spaniard)
(A crude insult based on the stereotypical view of greasy Latins. First coined in 1904 during the US construction of the Panama Canal, the word 'spick' is thought to be an abbreviation of the familiar Hispanic reply, 'No spic English.')

Oil tanker wanker

Oily rag fag (cigarette)

Old fogey bogey (snot)

Old iron and brass grass
(From the rag and bone man's collection call of 'any old iron', popularised by the 1911 music-hall song of that title performed by Harry Champion.)

Old King Cole the dole

Old oak the Smoke (London)
('The Smoke' has been London's nickname from the nineteenth century on account of its polluted atmosphere from homes and factories.)

Oliver Reed weed (cannabis)
(A 1960s rhyme usually shortened to 'olly' and characterising the lifestyle of the hell-raising English actor (1938–99).)

Oliver Twist pissed
(When it came to alcohol, Dickens's hero obviously shouldn't have asked for more.)

Omar Sharif grief
(After the smooth Egyptian actor, as in, 'Will you stop giving me so much Omar!')

On and off cough

On Golden Pond blonde
(The title of the 1981 film starring Henry Fonda is only used in connection with genuine blondes, not so-called aviation blondes – 'blonde hair, black box'.)

On the floor poor
(A rhyme reflecting where you might end up sleeping if you've got no money.)

One-time looker hooker
(A sad comment on how a girl's looks change as she drifts into drugs and prostitution.)

Ones and twos shoes

Ooh la la bra
(A hint of French naughtiness from the days when bras were considered risqué.)

Orange peel feel

Orange squash dosh (money)

Orchestra stalls balls (testicles)
(Shortened to 'orchestras' or, more usually, 'orks', as in, 'Stop playing with your orks while you're watching the KY jelly.')

Orphan Annie fanny (vagina)
(*Little Orphan Annie* was the title of a US comic strip created by Harold Gray that first appeared in 1924. Aimed primarily at children, its sense of innocence is in stark contrast to its rhyming slang meaning.)

Osama bin Laden pardon
(As in, 'I beg your Osama.')

Otis Redding wedding
(From the US soul singer (1941–67) who died in a plane crash.)

Oven mitts tits
(A rhyme acknowledging the difficulty of being tactile while wearing oven gloves.)

Overcoat maker undertaker
(A 'wooden overcoat' is a slang term for 'coffin'.)

Owen Nares chairs
(After the suave English actor (1888–1943) who was a matinee idol of the 1920s.)

Oxford bags fags (cigarettes)
(Based on the loose-fitting baggy trousers favoured by Oxford University students from the 1920s to the 1950s. Alarmingly they made a comeback in the 1970s – the decade that style forgot – when worn with platform shoes.)

Oxford scholar collar, dollar
(In the mid-nineteenth century there were about four US dollars to the pound sterling and so five shillings became known as a 'dollar', which in rhyming slang was converted to an 'Oxford scholar'.)

Oxo cube Tube (London Underground)
(Oxo concentrated meat extract was introduced in liquid form in 1899 and marketed as a cube from 1910. The cube has been rhyming slang for the London Underground since the late 1950s when its standing was enhanced by a long-running series of TV commercials featuring dutiful housewife Katie and her husband Philip, a man whose entire *raison d'être* seemed to revolve around gravy.)

Are you a real fridge freezer?

1. What part of your body is your jam tart?

2. If you had a Mars bar on your face, what would you see?

3. What type of drink is a magistrate's court?

4. Why might you sit on Lionel Blair?

5. Where would you be if you were in a flowery dell?

6. What would you be if you were Jimmy Shand?

7. How much money would you have if you had a macaroni?

8. What state would you be in if you were lord and mastered?

9. Which district of London is rhymed with 'arm'?

10. In rhyming slang, what is a la-di-da?

Answers: 1. Heart 2. Scar 3. A short 4. It's the rhyme for 'chair' 5. Prison cell 6. Banned 7. £25 (pony) 8. Plastered (drunk) 9. Chalk Farm 10. Cigar

P

Paddy and Mick pick, thick (stupid)
(A distinctly non-PC rhyme that captures the stereotypical image of slow-witted Irish labourers and is even extended to the tools they might use.)

Pain in the neck cheque
(Which it can be if you've got to write a large one, especially to your ex-wife or the Inland Revenue.)

Pair of kippers slippers
(The physical resemblance between two kippers and a pair of old slippers is undeniable – and unfortunately sometimes the smell is too.)

Pall Mall gal (girl)
(Long before Jimmy Savile smoked his first cigar or bought his first shell suit, it was commonplace to hear Cockneys refer to girls as 'gals'. The London street leading off Trafalgar Square served as the rhyme.)

Panoramas pyjamas
(A rhyme used chiefly by parents to encourage children in the 1950s to go to bed, as in, 'Come on, time to get your panoramas on.' Presumably the idea was that giving children the option of staying up to watch the BBC current affairs programme *Panorama* was the quickest way of getting them to go to bed.)

Pantomime cow row (argument)
(Few arguments can have such grave consequences as when the front end of a pantomime cow falls out with the back end... especially if the front end has just had a curry.)

Paper bag nag
(This can apply not only to a particularly slow horse but also to the sort of wife whose incessant complaining makes her so unattractive that her husband is tempted to put a paper bag over her head.)

Paper hat prat
(Perhaps derived from how people look when they wear one at Christmas.)

Paraffin lamp tramp
(Usually abbreviated to 'paraffin' in recognition of the liquid refreshment associated with down-and-outs.)

Paris Hilton Stilton (cheese)
(The hedonistic young socialite may be a big cheese in America but to many her behaviour takes the biscuit.)

Park benches Frenchies (the French)
(It's hard to imagine what the two have in common, except that both sit around a lot doing nothing. The biggest difference is that you can have a drink on a park bench but an Englishman rarely gets the chance to have a drink on a Frenchman.)

Partick Thistle whistle
(After the poor relations of Glasgow football whose lack of success led fan Billy Connolly to remark: 'I grew up thinking they were called Partick Thistle Nil.' So the referee's whistle invariably signalled another defeat.)

Pat Cash slash (urinate)
(The Australian tennis player rarely employed the backhand slash on his way to winning Wimbledon in 1987.)

Patsy Cline line (of cocaine)
(The US country music singer (1932–63) who guaranteed her immortality by being killed in a plane crash.)

Pattie Hearst first (degree result)
(The American heiress hit the headlines in 1974 when, after

being kidnapped by members of the Symbionese Liberation Army, she helped them rob a San Francisco bank.)

Paul McKenna tenner (£10)
(A modern rhyme about the British hypnotist who could wave a tenner in front of your eyes and convince you that you were a West Highland terrier.)

Paul Weller Stella (Artois)
(After the Woking-born musician – too many pints of 'Paul Weller' could put you in a jam with the law.)

Peace and quiet diet

Peanut butter nutter

Pearly Gate plate

Pearly King ring (anus)
(Dating back over a century, Pearly Kings and Queens are an essential part of the London tourist experience, along with Big Ben, red buses and bolshy taxi drivers. Therefore it goes without saying that they featured in *Mary Poppins*.)

Pea shooter hooter (nose)
(As in, 'That Barbra Streisand's got a pea shooter on her, hasn't she?')

Peas in the pot hot

Pebble-dashed smashed (drunk)
(In recognition of what often happens to the toilet bowl the morning after you've drunk a skinful.)

Pebble Mill pill
(A 1970s rhyme in memory of the former BBC Birmingham studios which opened in 1971 and produced more daytime chat shows than anyone would care to remember.)

Peckham Rye tie
(Dating from the nineteenth century and commemorating the thoroughfare in south-east London, this term has gained

such mainstream acceptance that there is even a tie manufacturer called Peckham Rye. In rhyming slang it is usually shortened to 'Peckham'.)

Pedigree Chum cum (semen)
(The association with a brand of dog food is not immediately apparent in this 1970s rhyme.)

Pen and ink stink
(First recorded in 1859, this rhyme was given a new lease of life by the 1980s TV series *Minder*, in which characters were frequently heard complaining about the 'pen and ink'. Sometimes abbreviated to 'pen'.)

Penny-a-mile tile (hat)
(A rhyme popular at the turn of the twentieth century when George Spartels wrote the music-hall song 'Where Did You Get That Hat?' with its opening lines of: 'Where did you get that hat, Where did you get that tile?')

Penny Black back
(The Penny Black was the name of the first British postage stamp, issued in 1840. The rhyme is often shortened to 'penny', so that a 'bad back' becomes a 'bad penny', obviously the sort that recurs.)

Penny locket pocket

Pepsi and Shirlie early
(After the 1980s singing duo (real names Helen DeMacque and Shirley Holliman) who started out as Wham!'s backing vocalists.)

Percy Sledge wedge (money)
(US soul singer whose biggest hit was the 1966 classic 'When A Man Loves A Woman'. The lyrics state that when a man loves a woman he would spend his very last dime on her, although the word 'wedge' usually refers to a wad of notes, as flashed about by Harry Enfield's 1980s character Loadsamoney.)

Percy Thrower blower (telephone)
(After the television gardening guru (1913–88), as in, 'Who was that on the Percy Thrower?')

Perry Como homo (gay man)
(A derogatory term for gay men, 'homo' paired up with the laid-back American singer (1912–2001) at the height of his fame in the fifties and sixties. Como himself was happily married to his childhood sweetheart Roselle for 65 years.)

Persian rugs drugs

Pete Tong wrong
(A Radio 1 disc jockey since 1991, Pete Tong has achieved the sort of fame that the likes of Tony Blackburn, Alan Freeman and Noel Edmonds could only dream of – a place in Cockney rhyming slang. The rhyme was originally thought to have been the brainchild of fellow DJ Mark Radcliffe but he has since given the credit to his former sidekick Marc 'Lard' Riley. A 2004 comedy film about a DJ who goes deaf was titled *It's All Gone Pete Tong*.)

Peter Brough up the duff (pregnant)
('Up the duff' first appeared in print as a euphemism for 'pregnant' in 1941 but its origins date back to the late nineteenth century when 'in the pudding club' also meant 'pregnant'. 'Duff' (a corruption of 'dough') was simply an alternative word for 'pudding'. The rhyme comes from the 1950s when Peter Brough (1916–99) was a major radio personality thanks to his dummy Archie Andrews who, being made of wood, was unlikely to get anyone up the duff. Brough, who apparently never saw the irony in being a radio ventriloquist, retired once television exposed his shortcomings, but by then *Educating Archie* had already provided first steps on the showbusiness ladder for the likes of Benny Hill, Tony Hancock, Dick Emery, Bruce Forsyth and 14-year-old Julie Andrews who played Archie's girlfriend.)

Peter O'Toole stool
(This refers mainly to a bar stool, a favourite perch for the notoriously thirsty Irish actor.)

Peter Pan can (safe), van
(Hence the confusing instruction from the leader of a gang of ram-raiders, 'Quick, get the Peter Pan into the Peter Pan!')

Peter Purves nervous
(On the contrary the presenter of *Blue Peter* from 1967 to 1979 always appeared an oasis of calm, even when Lulu the baby elephant did a sizeable wee on the studio floor and dragged her helpless keeper through the urine puddle or when fellow presenter John Noakes was knocked out by a five-pound imitation marrow.)

Peters and Lee pee
(Lennie Peters (1939–92) and Dianne Lee were an easy-listening duo who sprang to fame in the 1970s on the ITV talent show *Opportunity Knocks*. Their gimmick was that Lennie was blind, and they did much to improve the public's acceptance of disability. For when Peters and Lee came on the radio suddenly deafness didn't seem such a terrible prospect.)

Petrol pump hump
(The mood rather than the sexual activity, as in, 'You didn't 'arf have the petrol pump last night.')

Peyton Place face
(Based on the 1956 novel of the same title by Grace Metalious, *Peyton Place* entered Cockney consciousness in 1965 when it started a five-year run on British television as the first soap to be imported from the US. The tale of sexual shenanigans in a small New England town, it made stars of Mia Farrow and Ryan O'Neal.)

PG Tips lips
('You've got lovely PGs' might seem like a compliment – until you remember that the brand of tea is most readily associated with chimps.)

Phil the Fluter shooter (gun)
('Shooter' has been slang for 'gun' since the nineteenth century and is rhymed with the central character in the traditional Irish ballad 'Phil The Fluter's Ball'.)

Philharmonic gin and tonic

Photo finish Guinness
(The rhyme indicates the slurring of speech resulting from that telltale ninth pint.)

Piccadilly silly
(After the central London street situated in an area that was once known as Portugal but changed its name in the seventeenth century thanks to a local tailor named Robert Baker who specialised in making 'piccadils' – fashionable collars with lace borders.)

Pick and choose booze

Pick up sticks six

Pickled onion bunion
(As in, 'That's a nasty pickled onion you've got on your foot.')

Pie and liquor vicar

Pie and mash cash, slash (urinate)

Pieces of eight weight
(Usually condensed to 'pieces', as in, 'You're so fat, the back of your neck looks like a pack of hot dogs – isn't it time you did something about your pieces?')

Pig in the middle piddle
(After the popular children's game, in which constantly jumping to intercept the ball might exacerbate the need for the toilet. In rhyming slang the phrase is generally shortened to 'pig'.)

Pig's ear beer
(From the late nineteenth century and thus predating the

other (non-rhyming) slang use for 'pig's ear' meaning a 'cock-up'.)

Pig's trotter squatter

Pillar and post ghost
(The saying 'from pillar to post' started out life around 1420 as 'from post to pillar' and apparently refers to the pillars and posts that were part of the indoor courts used for the game of real tennis.)

Pimple and blotch Scotch (whisky)

Pin pegs legs
(Shortened to 'pins', as in, 'For his age Bruce Forsyth is still sprightly on his pins.' (See also **Rin Tin Tins**.))

Pineapple chapel

Pineapple chunk spunk (semen)
(As in, 'When I swallowed his pineapple, the man from Del Monte he say, "Y-e-e-s-s!"')

Pinky and Perky turkey
(After the singing puppet pigs (Perky was the one in the hat) who were such stars in the 1960s that an episode of their show titled 'You Too Can Be a Prime Minister' was banned by the BBC in 1966 for fear that it might influence the forth-coming general election.)

Pirates of Penzance pants
(From the Gilbert and Sullivan comic opera that premiered in 1879.)

Plate of ham gam (oral sex)
(Since the 1950s this has usually been shortened to 'plate', although in his diaries Kenneth Williams relates a typically scurrilous story about a gay man who got crabs in his mous-tache 'because of a plate of ham'.)

Plates of meat feet
(One of the best-known examples of Cockney rhyming slang, this term dates back to the nineteenth century, one of its first appearances in print being in 1887 when an edition of *Referee* included the lines: 'As she walked along the street with her little "plates of meat", And the summer sunshine falling, On her golden "Barnet Fair".' As with so many of the most popular rhymes, familiarity has seen it condensed to just 'plates'.)

Pleasure and pain rain

Plinkety plonk vin blanc (white wine)
(The rhyme in its entirety was first coined by Australian troops serving in France during the First World War and was subsequently reduced to 'plonk' as an uncomplimentary description for any cheap wine.)

Plymouth Argyles piles
(After the name of the Devon football club founded in 1886.)

Pogo stick prick (penis)
(According to legend the pogo stick was invented by a Burmese farmer who made one for his shoeless daughter so that she could hop all the way to pray daily at the nearest temple, but it was first manufactured commercially in 1919 by George Hansburg, an American toy designer. For the purposes of rhyming slang, it is usually shortened to 'pogo'.)

Polish and gloss toss (masturbate)
(A rhyme inspired by the manual exertion needed for both disciplines.)

Polly parrots carrots

Polo mint skint
(Introduced by Rowntree in 1948, Polo mints are so popular that if all the Polos produced every two hours were stacked on top of each other, they would form a six-mile-tall tower, higher than Mount Everest and considerably more difficult to climb.)

Pompey whore twenty-four
(An early twentieth-century expression that sprang up among Portsmouth sailors.)

Pony and trap the clap (gonorrhoea), crap
(The second meaning is the most common and is often shortened to 'pony', as in, 'I've never heard such a load of old pony!')

Poor relation station
(This rhyme originated in the early twentieth century when only the wealthy could afford cars, leaving everyone else to travel by train.)

Pop goes the weasel diesel
(From the seventeenth-century nursery rhyme, and fraught with potential hazards if a child asks his dad for a can of pop.)

Pork and bean queen (homosexual)

Pork chop cop
(No doubt inspired by the fact that 'pig' has been a derogatory term for a police officer since at least 1811.)

Pork pies lies
(First recorded in the 1980s but now so well established that it is frequently abbreviated to 'porkies'. A 'porky' tends to be a small fib rather than a downright whopper. For example, telling your girlfriend that you're going to have a quiet night in when really you're going out boozing with your mates would be termed a 'porky'; Tony Blair's dodgy dossier on the Iraq war would not.)

Porky Pig big
(The cartoon pig made his debut for Warner Bros in 1935. His trademark stutter came about because the original voice artist, Joe Dougherty, had one. However, Dougherty couldn't control his stutter, causing production costs to rise, and he was replaced in 1937 by Mel Blanc who went on to voice Porky for over 50 years. In rhyming slang 'Porky Pig' is not

only used with regard to an ample girth but also in an ironic sense, as in, 'I'm all glammed up and you're taking me to the Nag's Head tonight? That's porky pig of you!')

Port and brandy randy

Posh and Becks sex
(After Britain's premier celebrity couple, the thinking man's Peter Andre and Jordan. (See also **Victoria Beckham**.))

Pot and pan old man (husband or father)

Pot of glue clue

Potatoes in the mould cold
(A late nineteenth-century rhyme derived from the horticultural practice of covering potatoes still in the ground with a heap of earth to protect them from frost. The long-winded phrase has since been reduced to the more familiar 'taters', as in, 'It's taters in here. Shall I put the Ronan on?')

Pots and dishes wishes

Pound note coat

Pounds and pence sense

Pride and joy boy
(Every mother's pride and joy is her boy – until he brings home his first girlfriend.)

Puff and drag fag (cigarette)

Puff Daddy golf caddie
(A 1990s rhyme on the US rap artist, alias Sean Combs, alias P. Diddy, alias Diddy.)

Punch and Judy moody
(The traditional children's entertainment dates back to sixteenth-century Italy and a character called Punchinello who was then anglicised in the UK as Mr Punch in 1662. The story has been criticised for its violence but it does have a

moral: if you commit wholesale murder and repeatedly beat your wife, you will be eaten by a crocodile…although is probably more of a deterrent in Australia than Scotland.)

Parlez-vous Cockney?

I'm going down the poor relation to get the Oxo Pepsi and Shirlie tomorrow cos I'm up before the bubble at Big Ben and I don't want to be Harry Tate for the pogo.

(I'm going down the station to get the Tube early tomorrow cos I'm up before the beak at ten and I don't want to be late for the prick.)

Q

Quaker Oat coat
(After the US porridge-making company formed in 1901 and with a nod to the warmth provided by both a bowl of the cereal and an overcoat.)

Queen Mum bum
(In honour of Queen Elizabeth the Queen Mother (1900–2002) who, anti-royalists might claim, spent much of her life sitting on her bum.)

Queen Vic thick (stupid)
(The name of the Albert Square pub in *EastEnders*, an establishment where the Mitchell family set the intellectual tone. It must be the only pub in the country where Jade Goody could win quiz night.)

Queens Park Ranger stranger
(After the West London football club and first heard in the 1960s.)

Quentin Crisp lisp
(The outrageously homosexual Quentin Crisp (1908–99) became an author, raconteur and gay icon after changing his name from the less exotic Denis Pratt. His 1970s memoir *The Naked Civil Servant* (John Hurt played him in the TV adaptation) cemented his fame. Crisp was also the subject of Sting's song 'An Englishman In New York'.)

R

Rabbit and pork talk
(Since its inception around 1941, this rhyme has entered mainstream dialect to such an extent that it has not only been shortened to 'rabbit' but has even acquired its own spin-off, 'bunny'. Its finest hour to date was undoubtedly Chas and Dave's 1980 hit 'Rabbit' in which the Cockney duo sang about a girl who was an incessant talker and had 'more rabbit than Sainsbury's'. The word 'bunny' was repeated over and over again in the chorus.)

Rabbit hutch crotch (groin)

Radio Ones runs (diarrhoea)
(From the BBC's pop music station, which began broadcasting in 1967. An apt choice as, particularly in the Smashie and Nicey days of the 1970s and 1980s, many of its disc jockeys seemed to suffer from verbal diarrhoea.)

Radio Rental mental
(Based on the name of TV rental firm Radio Rentals, this rhyme first appeared in the 1970s. It is sometimes shortened to 'radio', as in, 'You wanna go to Margate on a day like this? Have you gone ravin' radio?')

Rag and bone throne (toilet)
(This refers to the sort of throne on which the Queen sits daily to wipe away the royal wee.)

Raging thirst first (degree result)
(Perhaps an ironic rhyme since any student who has a raging thirst for three years (i.e. spends most of his or her time in the campus bar) is unlikely to obtain a first.)

Raleigh bike dyke (lesbian)
(A particularly cutting rhyme since Nottingham cycle manufacturers Raleigh were famous for creating the 'Chopper',
which in its slang sense is just about the last thing a lesbian
would want to see.)

Randolph Scott spot
(From the US actor (1903–87), a celluloid Western hero of
the 1940s. Often squeezed to 'Randolphs', as in, 'That's one
hell of a Randolph you've got on your Errol!')

Rant and rave shave

Raquel Welch belch
(The glamorous American actress would seem just about the
least likely person on earth to let out a full-blooded belch.)

Rasher and bubble double (in darts)
(From the cheap dish of bacon and bubble and squeak,
which is leftover mashed potatoes and cabbage. (See also
Bubble and squeak.))

Raspberry ripple cripple, nipple
(Raspberry ripple was the new ice-cream taste sensation of
the 1960s and an obvious choice to rhyme with women's
nipples, which were becoming more visible with each passing year. The fact that raspberries are also firm, red fruits is
probably more than just coincidence. The phrase is often
shortened to 'raspberries', as in, 'She can't be wearing a
Roseanne – look at her raspberries!')

Raspberry tart fart
(Blowing raspberries to make a farting sound has been a
playground pursuit since the nineteenth century and was
elevated to an art form in the 1950s by *The Goon Show*'s Harry
Secombe. In 1976 his fellow Goon Spike Milligan wrote the
comic serial *The Phantom Raspberry Blower of Old London Town*
for *The Two Ronnies*. The word 'tart' has now become almost
superfluous to the rhyme, so that a 'raspberry' alone is sufficient to denote a loud breaking of wind.)

Rat trap Jap (Japanese)
(A British Second World War term and not surprisingly shortened to 'rat' at a time when hostilities between the nations were at their peak.)

Rats and mice rice
(When Chinese takeaways first hit Britain in the late 1960s, the stereotypical view of Little Englanders was that the restaurant kitchens were rife with rats and mice and that any rodents which survived the hygiene made it on to the menu.)

Rattle and clank bank

Rattle and hum cum (semen)

Ravi Shankar wanker
(From the Indian sitar player.)

Ray Mears beers
(A twenty-first-century entry in recognition of the British broadcaster and expert on survival techniques who surely welcomes a cold beer at the end of a hard day in the jungle.)

Read and write fight

Red hots the trots (diarrhoea)
(A rhyme speculating on the after effects of a vindaloo.)

Reeling and rocking stocking
(A rhyme from the rock 'n' roll era when fashions were becoming more daring; taken from the title of Chuck Berry's 1958 track 'Reelin' And Rockin'.)

Reg Varney Pakistani
(The star of seventies sitcom *On the Buses* has seen the number 11 rerouted way beyond Cemetery Gates.)

Reggie and Ronnie johnny (condom)
(Named after 1960s London gangland bosses Reggie (1933–2000) and Ronnie (1933–95) Kray, known affectionately

as 'the twins'. The rhyme is inspired by the fact that, like a condom, the Krays offered protection.)

Rhubarb crumble grumble

Rhythm and blues shoes

Ribbon and curl girl

Richard and Judy moody
(The husband-and-wife daytime chat show hosts have recently stood in for Punch and Judy in rhyming slang (see **Punch and Judy**). The bickering between Madeley and Finnigan may not be quite as fierce as between Mr Punch and his spouse but given Richard's tendency to spout garbage you can't blame Judy for occasionally appearing moody.)

Richard Burtons curtains
(The association with the noted Welsh actor (1925–84) suggests that 'Richard Burtons' may have originated with theatre curtains but have since grown to include the domestic variety too.)

Richard Gere beer
(After the American leading man and used in its entirety to avoid any unfortunate confusion with the 'Richard' below (see **Richard the Third**).)

Richard the Third bird (girl), turd
(King of England from 1483–85, Richard III suffered a bad press for centuries mainly because of the suspicion that he had arranged for the two young princes who were the rightful heirs to the throne to be murdered in the Tower of London. Then just as scholars started to clear his name, he became rhymed with a lump of excrement. It can be a cruel world – and also for any girl referred to as a 'Richard'. Would you really want to be compared to someone with Machiavellian tendencies, a pudding-basin haircut and a withered shoulder?)

Richard Todd cod
(After the British actor, as in, 'I'll have a Richard Todd and a portion of Jaggers, please.')

Ricky Gervais ace (playing cards)
(From the star of 1990s comedy series *The Office*, in which his character, David Brent, always saw himself as the joker.)

Riddick Bowe B.O.
(The former world heavyweight boxing champion obviously worked up a sweat in the ring.)

Riff raff Taff (Welsh)

Rifle range change (money)

Rink-a-dink Chink (Chinese)
(A politically incorrect rhyme from the 1970s when virtually every street seemed to have a 'rinky takeaway'.)

Rinky dink pink (snooker ball)

Rin Tin Tins pins (legs)
(German Shepherd dog Rin Tin Tin – affectionately known as 'Rinty' – was a movie star from the 1920s and a TV star in the 1950s, a long career explained by the fact that he was played by several different dogs. Athletic though he was, few girls are likely to appreciate having their legs compared to Rin Tin Tins, particularly as he had four of them. (See also **Pin pegs**.))

Rio Ferdinand grand (£1,000)
(After the Manchester United and England defender who reportedly gets paid over 120 Rio a week.)

Rip and tear swear

Rip Van Winkle tinkle (pee)
(Created in an 1819 short story by US author Washington Irving, Rip Van Winkle is best known for having gone to sleep for twenty years, which means he must have had an extraordinarily strong bladder.)

Rising damp cramp
(Probably from the manner in which rising damp creeps up walls and cramp can creep up your leg. The phrase enjoyed a new lease of life with Eric Chappell's 1970s comedy series starring Leonard Rossiter as seedy landlord Rigsby.)

River Nile denial
(As in, 'He just won't admit it – I'm afraid he's in the River Nile.')

River Ouse booze

River Tyne wine
(If there had really been wine in the River Tyne, wouldn't Gazza have drunk it dry years ago?)

Roast beef teeth

Roast pork fork

Rob Roy boy
(An obsolete rhyme in recognition of Scottish outlaw Rob Roy McGregor (1671–1734), sometimes known as the Scottish Robin Hood and hero of Walter Scott's 1818 novel *Rob Roy*.)

Roberta Flack sack
(The name of the American singer not only signifies job dismissal but also the colloquial meaning of 'sack' as 'bed', as in, 'I'm barb-wired, I'm going to hit the Roberta.')

Robin Hood good
(Although the song 'Robin Hood' insists that the legendary medieval outlaw of Sherwood Forest was 'feared by the bad, loved by the good', it is doubtful whether he was that much of a philanthropist – that's assuming he ever existed. To emphasise this, the rhyme is mainly used in a negative manner, as in, 'What did you buy that for? That's no Robin Hood!')

Robinson and Cleaver fever
(After a draper's store that opened in London's Regent Street at the end of the nineteenth century. The original Belfast

branch, specialising in Irish linen, was that city's grandest store at the time of the launch of the *Titanic* in 1912.)

Rock 'n' roll dole

Rock of ages wages
(Based on the title of the popular hymn written by Revd Augustus Montague Toplady and first published in 1775. The phrase entered rhyming slang in the 1930s and is often shortened to 'rocks'.)

Rockford Files piles
(Centred on private detective Jim Rockford (played by James Garner), *The Rockford Files* was a quirky US cop show that ran on British TV from 1975 to 1982. Garner suffered greatly for his art, finishing up with torn ligaments, sprains, dodgy knees, disc trouble and dislocations as a result of doing all his own stunts. About the only thing he didn't have was piles. The rhyme gained fresh impetus in the 1990s thanks to the comedy series *The Royle Family*, in which head of the house Jim Royle complained about having trouble with his 'Rockford Files'.)

Rocking horse sauce

Rocks and boulders shoulders

Rogan Josh dosh (money)
(A 1990s rhyme cooked up by lovers of the aromatic curry dish.)

Roger Mellie telly
(Roger Mellie, the man on the telly, is a strip cartoon character in the satirical magazine *Viz*, which began publication in 1979. A foul-mouthed TV presenter, his catchphrase is, with shades of David Frost, 'Hello, good evening and bollocks.')

Roger Moore door
(Unkind critics might suggest that the rhyme works because the former James Bond has the acting range of the average door.)

Rogue and villain shilling
(First recorded in 1859, the term continued doing the rounds right up until the shilling – the equivalent of 5p – was withdrawn in 1971.)

Rolf Harris arris (arse)
(A rhyme once removed commemorates the much-loved Australian entertainer, artist and world's leading exponent of the wobble board (see **Aristotle** and **Bottle and glass**).)

Roller coaster toaster

Rolls-Royce choice
(An apt rhyme because if they could afford it, a lot of people would plump for a Rolls-Royce as their car of choice.)

Roman candles sandals
(Taken from the fireworks that have lit up 5 November for decades, and particularly fitting as sandals were the favoured footwear of the Romans.)

Romantic ballad salad

Ronan Keating central heating
(Countless women would love to turn on the Irish solo singer and former member of Boyzone.)

Ronnie Biggs digs (lodgings)
(A member of the gang who pulled off the Great Train Robbery of 1963 and then escaped after serving just fifteen months in jail. He ended up in Brazil where he lived openly for many years before running out of money and returning to Britain in 2001 at the age of 71 to resume his 30-year sentence.)

Roof rack back

Rookery Nook book
(From the title of the 1923 novel written by Ben Travers (1886–1980) and subsequently adapted into a popular stage farce.)

Rory O'Moore door, floor
(A fictitious, all-purpose Irish character from the nineteenth century.)

Roseanne Barr bra
(The big-bosomed American comedian's series *Roseanne* ran from 1988 to 1997, winning a number of awards, and her bra should have been nominated for Best Support.)

Rosie Lee tea
(The identity of the original Rosie Lee remains a mystery but the rhyme bearing her name is believed to have originated around the time of the First World War, thus comfortably predating American stripper Gypsy Rose Lee who did not achieve prominence until the late 1930s. The rhyme is often contracted to 'Rosie' and has gained such worldwide recognition that an English-themed tea shop in New York markets its own blend of black tea called Rosie Lee.)

Rosie O'Grady's ladies' (toilet)

Round the houses trousers
(Originating in the mid-nineteenth century, as in, 'Quick, my Teletubby's coming. Out the Tommy Trinder and don't forget your round the houses.')

Roy Castle arsehole
(No slight intended on the versatile entertainer (1932–94) but his surname just happened to have a convenient rhyme.)

Roy Hudds spuds (potatoes)
(After the veteran actor, comedian and expert on all things related to the music hall.)

Royal Mail bail

Rub-a-dub pub, sub (pay advance)
('Rub-a-dub' has been used as a rhyme for 'pub' since the early twentieth century and is generally abbreviated to 'rubber', as in, 'Fancy popping down the rubber for a quick one?')

Rubber duck fuck

Rubik's Cubes pubes (pubic hair)
(The puzzle was invented in 1974 by Hungarian Ernö Rubik, who called it the Magic Cube, but it was renamed Rubik's Cube for its commercial launch in 1980. Over the next two years 100 million Rubik's Cubes were sold, making it the world's most popular toy. Although there are billions of different permutations, some anoraks can solve it in nine seconds.)

Ruby Murray curry
(Even though her heyday was the 1950s, Irish singer Ruby Murray (1935–96) was still reasonably fresh in the public's minds when the great curry boom hit Britain in the early seventies. She has since fought off challenges from actor Bill Murray, comedian Al Murray and even tennis player Andy Murray to remain the undisputed queen of curry, a position acknowledged by the fact that a curry is often just referred to as a 'Ruby'.)

Ruby red head

Rudolf Hess mess
(Hitler's deputy (1894–1987) got himself into a right old Rudolf in 1941 when he flew solo to Scotland in an apparent attempt to negotiate peace with Britain. Parachuting from his plane south of Glasgow, he broke his ankle on landing and was promptly arrested by a local farmer and thrown into jail for the next 46 years.)

Ruin and spoil oil

Runner and rider cider

Runner bean Queen (Elizabeth II)

Rupert Bears flares (trousers), shares
(Created by English artist Mary Tourtel, Nutwood's most famous resident made his debut in a strip cartoon in the *Daily Express* in 1920. In those distinctive checked trousers, he was an obvious choice to represent flares and in the 1980s

he also infiltrated the London Stock Exchange where shares were frequently called 'Ruperts', the name itself conveying an instant image of chinless yuppie stockbrokers.)

Russell Crowe dough (money)
(Based on the volatile Australian actor, as in, 'So how much Russell Crowe are you getting paid for this film?')

Russell Harty party
(After the idiosyncratic, Lancashire-born TV chat show host (1934–88) whose series *Russell Harty Plus* debuted on ITV in 1973. His most memorable contribution to the history of television was being slapped in the face by singer Grace Jones on a live edition of his 1980s BBC show.)

Rusty nail jail

Ruud Gullit bullet
(A rhyme coined after the former Dutch international footballer got the bullet as manager of Chelsea in 1998.)

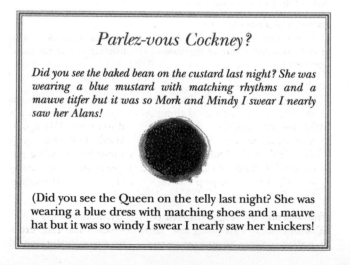

Parlez-vous Cockney?

Did you see the baked bean on the custard last night? She was wearing a blue mustard with matching rhythms and a mauve titfer but it was so Mork and Mindy I swear I nearly saw her Alans!

(Did you see the Queen on the telly last night? She was wearing a blue dress with matching shoes and a mauve hat but it was so windy I swear I nearly saw her knickers!

S

S Club 7 heaven
(A twenty-first-century rhyme in memory of the manufactured boy/girl pop group who had to change their name to S Club after one member left.)

Sad and sorry lorry
(Which of course you would be if you were run over by one.)

Safe and sound ground
(This reflects the relative security felt by being on the ground as opposed, for example, to riding in a hot-air balloon. However, this rhyme tends to lose some of its validity during an earthquake.)

Saint and sinner dinner
(A religious nineteenth-century term giving thanks to the Lord for food while at the same time hinting at the perils of gluttony.)

Sally Gunnell tunnel
(Essex girls are renowned for coming first but Chigwell-born Sally Gunnell outstripped them all by winning the women's 400 metres hurdles at the 1992 Barcelona Olympics. Commentators reckoned that she would have won even more easily if she had taken off her white stilettos. Although her performance as a TV athletics presenter was widely panned, she is still popular in rhyming slang, referencing either the Blackwall or Dartford Tunnel.)

Salmon and trout gout, snout (tobacco), stout (beer)
('Snout' has been slang for 'tobacco' since the late nineteenth century and soon gave rise to the rhyme 'salmon and

trout', or 'salmon' for short. Recently young Londoners modified it to mean 'cigarette', as in, 'Oi, mate, have you got a salmon on you?')

Salvation Army barmy
(After the Christian charity founded by William Booth in London's East End in 1865.)

Samantha Janus anus
(The British actress who has starred in *EastEnders* and had the misfortune to represent the UK in the 1991 Eurovision Song Contest (she finished equal tenth with 'A Message To Your Heart') has become so fed up with rhymes about her surname that she insists it is pronounced 'Jannus'.)

Samantha Mumba number
(From the Irish singer/songwriter, as in, 'Hey, gorgeous, can I have your Samantha?')

Samuel Pepys creeps
(From the celebrated London diarist (1633–1703), as in, 'This place gives me the Samuels.')

Sandy Powell towel
(A more palatable alternative to Enoch (see **Enoch Powell**) is this rhyme commemorating the red-haired, Yorkshire-born music-hall comedian (1898–1982) whose catchphrase was 'Can you hear me, mother?' Well, it was probably funny at the time.)

Santa's grotto blotto (drunk)
('Blotto' has been a slang term for 'very drunk' since the First World War and this rhyme suggests that the red cheeks of department-store Santas owe more to a hip flask than a naturally rosy complexion.)

Satin and silk milk

Saucepan handle candle

Saucepan lid kid
(Although this can be used in the sense of 'to kid' meaning 'to fool', its most common form since the 1960s has been with reference to children, as in that familiar cry of an estranged husband, 'Is it all right if I take the saucepan lids to the zoo on Sunday?')

Sausage and mash cash, crash
(Cockneys have been using one of their favourite dishes to describe money since the late nineteenth century. The rhyme is often shortened to 'sausage' and may have some connection with the phrase 'not a sausage' meaning 'absolutely nothing'.)

Sausage roll dole, Pole
(As in, with regard to John Paul II, 'That was a turn-up, having a sausage roll as Pope.')

Savoury rissole pisshole
(A savoury dish yields an unsavoury rhyme.)

Scapa Flow go
(Whereas rhyming slang sometimes throws up words that become colloquialisms in their own right (e.g. 'potatoes in the mould'>'taters'), this one worked in reverse. Coming from the Italian *scappare* (meaning 'to escape'), 'scarper' has been a slang expression for a hurried departure since the 1840s. Yet it was not until the First World War, when the Scapa Flow naval base in the Orkneys played a key role in the defence of the nation, that 'Scapa Flow' emerged as rhyming slang for 'go' with an obvious nod to the already existing 'scarper'.)

Schindler's List pissed
(A rhyme for film buffs taken from the title of Steven Spielberg's award-winning 1993 movie adapted from Thomas Keneally's novel *Schindler's Ark*. Liam Neeson starred as Oskar Schindler, a German businessman who saved over 1,000 Polish Jews during the Holocaust. The flippant rhyme is usually shortened to 'Schindler's', as in, 'I'm

not surprised you don't remember much about last night –
you were well Schindler's.')

Scooby-Doo clue
(The cowardly Great Dane who has featured in Hanna-
Barbera cartoons since 1969. Each week he joined a team of
teenage detectives – Shaggy, Fred, Daphne and Velma – in
solving ghostly goings-on. The rhyme is neat because
although Scooby was always supposed to be searching for
clues, he didn't really have one.)

Scotch eggs legs
(A highly descriptive rhyme if your legs happen to be short,
oval-shaped and coated in breadcrumbs.)

Scotch mist pissed

Scotch pegs legs
(Dating from the mid-nineteenth century and usually abbreviated to 'scotches'.)

Scuba diver fiver

Sebastian Coes toes
(A relevant rhyme because few people could 'have it on their
Sebs' ('make a quick getaway') faster than the man who won
1,500 metres gold at both the 1980 and 1984 Olympics.)

Seek and search church
(Maybe a rhyme inspired by the tale of a reluctant groom.)

Selina Scott spot
(Presenter Selina Scott filled many TV spots in the 1980s
boasting what appeared to be either an immaculate complexion or the work of an excellent make-up artist.)

Semolina cleaner
(From the grim dessert that was a mainstay of school dinners
in the 1950s, as in, 'Are you still working as a semolina down
the Rose and Crown?')

September Morn horn (erection)
(The title of a 1912 painting by Frenchman Paul Chabas (1669–1937) depicting a young woman bathing in the nude. When it was displayed in the window of a Chicago art gallery in 1913, the city's mayor took exception and charged the gallery owner with indecency. The resulting court case, which the gallery owner won, ensured the painting's notoriety although it was another 60 years before it entered rhyming slang.)

Septic tank Yank
(Although first coined by Australians in the 1960s, this derogatory term for Americans has since won international approval. For good measure 'anti-septic' – sometimes in the form of 'Listerine' – means 'anti-American'.)

Seven Dials piles
(Seven Dials is a junction in London's Covent Garden where seven narrow streets converge. It takes its name from the column in the centre of the junction which has a sundial with six faces, the story being that the seventh dial is formed by the column itself casting a shadow on the ground. In the nineteenth and early twentieth centuries, the Seven Dials area was synonymous with crime and poverty, prompting Agatha Christie to pen *The Seven Dials Mystery* in 1929.)

Sexton Blake cake, fake
(Written by Harry Blyth under the pen-name of 'Hal Meredith', Sexton Blake was a fictional English detective who made his debut in *The Halfpenny Marvel* magazine in 1893. Blake was sometimes considered a pale version of Sherlock Holmes (the two men were of similar build, both had offices in London's Baker Street and both relied on the services of a housekeeper) so perhaps it is no surprise that he has been rhymed chiefly with 'fake'. Cockney art forger Tom Keating used to call his 2,000-plus copies of the works of the great masters his 'Sexton Blakes'.)

Shake and shiver river

Shakin' Stevens evens (betting odds)
(After the Welsh rock 'n' roll revivalist (real name Michael Barratt) who enjoyed chart success in the early 1980s.)

Shania Twain pain
(The Canadian singer/songwriter sometimes complains that her femininity is a pain because it gets in the way of her music. She should buy a longer guitar strap.)

Sharleen Spiteri hairy
(It could be the Mediterranean family background (her father is of Maltese descent) that has led to the Scottish singer with soft rock band Texas being rhymed with 'hairy'. Even so, it is preferable to the nickname thrown up by her surname at school – 'Spit the Dog' after Bob Carolgees's gobbing mutt on *Tiswas*.)

Sharon Stone phone (mobile)
(After the Hollywood actress, as in, 'When are you going to get off the Sharon Stone?')

Shaun Ryder cider
(It requires no great leap of the imagination to conclude that the lead singer of Manchester band the Happy Mondays has enjoyed the odd glass or two of cider in his time.)

Shepherd's pie sky
(Probably connected to the amateur weather forecasters' rhyme: 'Red sky at night shepherd's delight, Red sky in the morning shepherd's warning.')

Sherbet Dab cab

Sherbet Dip kip

Sherman tank wank
(From the Second World War US tank named after US General William T. Sherman (1820–91). Usually reduced to 'Sherman'.)

Shillings and pence sense
(As in, 'Your brother hasn't got the shillings he was born with.')

Shiny and bright all right

Shirley Bassey chassis
(The Welsh diva still has an enviable 'chassis' even though she is now in her seventies.)

Shout and holler collar

Shovel and pick nick (prison)
(A reference to the tools used by prison gangs in the days before hard labour was replaced by a games room and wide-screen TV.)

Shovels and spades AIDS
(A grim reminder of the consequences of contracting the deadly disease.)

Sighs and tears ears

Sigourney Weaver beaver (female genital area)
(After the US actress, as in, 'I wouldn't mind getting a butcher's of her Sigourney.')

Silas Hockings stockings
(In memory of English novelist Silas Hocking (1850–1935) whose second book, *Her Benny* (1879), a story of Liverpool street children, sold over a million copies.)

Silver and gold old

Silver spoon moon

Simon Cowells bowels
(A fitting rhyme for the man who has made a career out of scraping the bottom of the music barrel.)

Simon Schamas pyjamas
(After the British TV historian.)

Simply shocking stocking
(Mocking the old establishment view that too much thigh shown at the top of a lady's stocking would corrupt the nation's morals and lead to the end of civilisation as we know it.)

Sinbad the Sailor tailor
(From the seafaring hero in *The Arabian Nights* stories.)

Sinead O'Connor doner (kebab)
(Once Turkish fast food hit Britain in the 1980s it was only a matter of time before a suitable rhyming donor was found. Step forward Irish songstress Sinead O'Connor who, being a vegan, was almost certainly horrified by the connection.)

Sistine Chapel apple
(After the chapel in the papal palace in Rome's Vatican City, famous for its ornate ceiling by Michelangelo. Somehow it seems wasted on an apple.)

Sit beside her spider
(From the nursery rhyme 'Little Miss Muffet', first published in 1805, and which contains the line: 'Along came a spider who sat down beside her.' It also conjures up images of old-style outside toilets where the act of pulling the chain could make several families of spiders homeless.)

Six and eight straight

Six to four whore
(A 1950s rhyme supposedly based on the odds of picking up an infection from a visit to a prostitute.)

Skin and blister sister
(A rhyme originating in the 1920s, as in, 'Is your skin and blister still going out with that geezer with the wonky minces?')

Sky rocket pocket
(First recorded in the nineteenth century and still heard today. The term is often shortened to 'sky'.)

Skylark park (a vehicle)

Skyscraper paper

Slap and tickle pickle
(Possibly because you'd be in a pickle if your partner caught you enjoying a bit of slap and tickle with someone else. 'Slap and tickle' has been a euphemism for lively foreplay since the 1920s. The band Squeeze exploited the unsuitability of pickles as an aphrodisiac in their 1979 song 'Slap And Tickle', which contained the lines: 'Never chew a pickle, With a little slap and tickle.')

Slim Shady old lady
(After American rap artist Eminem's alter ego, as in, 'Wait there, I'm just going to help that Slim Shady across the road.')

Slippery Sid yid (Jew)

Slug and snail fingernail

Smack in the eye pie
(Which could lead to some confusion if someone asks you, 'Do you want a smack in the eye?')

Smash and grab cab
(A thinly veiled accusation that taxi fares are daylight robbery.)

Smear and smudge judge

Smile and smirk work
(Often shortened to 'smile', as in, 'All smile and no Evelyn makes Jack a dull boy.')

Snake's hiss piss

Snow and ice price

Snow Whites tights
(Maybe it was seeing the Brothers Grimm fairytale heroine with her tights around her ankles that made one of her little friends Bashful.)

Soap and lather father
(A late nineteenth-century rhyme mirroring Dad's morning shave.)

Soap and water daughter

Sodom and Gomorrah borrow
(According to the Book of Genesis, Sodom and Gomorrah were the two cities destroyed by God for their sinful reputations. Brighton might suffer similar retribution today. By contrast the virtuous inhabitants of Eastbourne would be preserved for centuries – and indeed look as if they have been. The rhyme works because of the Cockney pronunciation 'borrer'.)

Soldier bold cold
(An old military rhyme reminiscent of Private Pike in *Dad's Army* wrapped up in his woolly scarf on parade because his mum didn't want him to catch cold.)

Somerset Maugham warm
(After the English writer (1874–1965).)

Son and daughtered slaughtered (drunk)

Sonny and Cher pair
(The US singing duo of Sonny Bono (1935–98) and his wife Cher appeared the perfect pop pair in 1965 when they topped the charts with 'I Got You Babe', but ten years later the partnership ended in an acrimonious divorce. Sonny turned to politics and Scientology and died after skiing into a tree; Cher is still going strong in her sixties although with her fondness for cosmetic surgery, hardly any of her original parts are left.)

Sooty and Sweep on the cheap
(Created by the late, great Harry Corbett (1918–89), Sooty and Sweep bestrode children's television for more than 50 years like glove-puppet colossi. Sooty was certainly bought on the cheap – amateur magician Corbett paid 7s 6d for the

puppet on a wet family holiday in Blackpool in 1948 to keep his children amused. Sooty and Sweep appeared in Peter Kay's 2005 video for '(Is This The Way To) Amarillo' and Sooty's legions of famous fans include Iron Maiden drummer Nicko McBrain who has the orange bear on the front of his drumkit.)

Sorry and sad bad

South Pole arsehole
(Geographical similarities between the two, the main difference being that not many people have a Norwegian flag sticking out of their arsehole.)

Southend beach speech

Southend Piers ears
(A particularly appropriate rhyme for anyone with protruding ears – Dumbo, Mr Spock, Gary Lineker – since Southend Pier is almost a mile and a half long.)

Spam fritter shitter (anus)
(Spam – it stands for shoulder pork and ham – was created in 1937 and, as a regular component of servicemen's rations, was widely credited with helping the Allies win the Second World War. A Dorset boy became addicted to it – eating six tins a week for three years – while a horde of Vikings on *Monty Python's Flying Circus* took time off from raping and pillaging to sing the praises of Spam. The Spam fritter (a slice of Spam fried in batter) is so synonymous with the war that the British government suggested cooking thousands of them in 1995 to commemorate the 50th anniversary of VE Day.)

Spanish guitar cigar

Spanish Main drain
(From the name by which the seas in the Caribbean were known between the sixteenth and eighteenth centuries. Often reduced to 'Spanish', as in, 'That new jamjar is just money down the Spanish.'

Spanish waiter potato

Spare rib fib

Sparrow bow and arrow
(From the nursery rhyme 'Who Killed Cock Robin?' (see **Bow and arrow**).)

Sporting Life wife
(A British racing newspaper (1859–1998) behind which many a wife could find her husband, especially on a Saturday morning.)

Spotted dick sick
(And you would be if you had one, although the rhyme is actually named after the suet pudding dotted with raisins.)

Squad halt salt
(A military rhyme popular during the First World War.)

Squadron Leader Biggles giggles
(The daredevil British pilot and boys' own hero was created by author W. E. Johns in 1932 and went on to feature in nearly 100 books. For the sake of his reputation it is to be hoped that Biggles's chum Ginger was not also dipped in rhyming slang. (See **Ginger beer**.))

Sri Lanka wanker

St Louis blues shoes

Stage fright light (ale)
(A comment on the nerve-calming qualities of a beer before a performance.)

Stamford Bridge fridge
(In honour of the home ground of Chelsea Football Club, where, until the Abramovich revolution, the fridge contained more cups than the trophy cabinet.)

Stammer and stutter butter

Stan and Ollie brolly (umbrella)
(After comedy movie duo Stan Laurel (1890–1965) and
Oliver Hardy (1892–1957) for whom the simple act of open-
ing an umbrella would be the prelude to chaos and disaster.
(See also **Laurel and Hardy**.))

Stand at ease cheese

Stand to attention pension

Stars and Garters tomatoes
(After the title of the 1960s ITV variety show set in a fake
London pub and hosted by Ray Martine and his pet mynah
bird.)

Starsky and Hutch clutch, crotch (groin)
('Good buddy' TV cops Dave Starsky (played by Paul
Michael Glaser) and Ken Hutchinson (David Soul) somehow epitomised the 1970s – screeching cars, dodgy music
and even worse fashions. The first rhyme stems from their
red and white 1974 Ford Torino; the second was probably
based on Soul's sex-symbol status at the time.)

Steam tug mug (fool)
(Invariably shortened to 'steamer', as in, 'Fancy falling for
that old trick! What a steamer!')

Steely Dan tan
(Founded by Donald Fagen and Walter Becker, New York
jazz/rock band Steely Dan took their name from a steam-
powered dildo that featured in William Burroughs's 1959
novel *Naked Lunch*.)

Steffi Graf laugh
(A 1990s rhyme based on German tennis player Steffi Graf
who won the Wimbledon ladies' singles title seven times
between 1988 and 1996.)

Steve Claridge garage
(A journeyman striker who played in English League football
from 1984 to 2007 – his many clubs included Birmingham

City, Leicester City and Millwall – and was renowned for his gambling habit, dishevelled appearance and clapped-out motor, which was invariably in the garage if not abandoned by the roadside.)

Steve McQueens jeans
(In memory of the US movie star (1930–80), nicknamed the 'King of Cool'.)

Stevie Nicks flicks (cinema)
(After the American singer best known for her work with Fleetwood Mac in the 1970s.)

Stevie Wonder chunder (vomit), thunder
(The blind American singer/songwriter (born Steveland Judkins) who had his first hit at thirteen and whose career even survived a duet with Paul McCartney.)

Stewart Granger danger
(From the English actor (1913–93) often associated with heroic roles.)

Stewed prune tune

Sticks and stones bones
(From the familiar playground response to a verbal insult: 'Sticks and stones may break my bones, but names will never hurt me.')

Sticky toffee coffee

Stinging nettle kettle

Stockport County Bounty (bar)
(There is a nagging feeling that the coconut-filled chocolate bar might not have caught on with the slogan: 'Stockport – the taste of paradise.')

Stoke-on-Trent bent (gay)

Stone jug mug (fool)

Stop and start heart
(An alarming rhyme that sounds like a scene from *Casualty*.)

Strange and weird beard
(An indication of the suspicion with which facial hair is regarded by some people – and understandably so. After all, Saddam Hussein, Osama bin Laden, Dave Lee Travis: besides their crimes against humanity, what was the other thing they had in common?)

Strawberry split git

Strawberry tart heart
(A puzzling rhyme until it is shortened to 'strawberry' and the visual connection becomes clear.)

String vest pest
(The string vest was invented in 1933 by Norwegian army commandant Henrik Brun who sewed together the first garment from old fishing nets. Its heyday was in the 1950s when it was popularised by the likes of strip cartoon character Andy Capp (see **Andy Capp**). Builders and the comic Glaswegian philosopher Rab C. Nesbitt attempted to keep it alive but recently Asda announced that the string vest market had unravelled to the extent that the store would no longer be stocking them.)

Struggle and strain train
(A rhyme that perfectly sums up rail travel in modern Britain.)

Stutter and stammer hammer

Sue Lawley poorly
(After the former BBC television newsreader and presenter of radio's *Desert Island Discs* (1988–2006).)

Sugar and spice ice, nice
(The second meaning comes from the old rhyme claiming that little girls are made of 'sugar and spice and all things nice'. Not when you pulled their pigtails they weren't.)

Sunday roast post

Surrey Docks pox
(From the Thames-side area of Rotherhithe that served as a dockyard from 1696 to 1969. The district has now been given the more upmarket name of Surrey Quays.)

Suzie Wong pong (smell)
(Hong Kong hooker Suzie Wong was the unlikely heroine of *The World of Suzie Wong,* a 1957 novel by Richard Mason that three years later was turned into a film starring William Holden.)

Swallow and sigh collar and tie
(Possibly based on what you might do if your tie is too tight.)

Swanee River liver
(The Suwanee River flows from Georgia to the Gulf of Mexico and in 1851 inspired Stephen C. Foster to write 'The Swanee River' (he misspelled the name), which in 1935 was adopted as the state song of Florida.)

Swear and cuss bus
(This of course is what you do while waiting for a London bus, which, for safety reasons, habitually travel in threes.)

Sweaty sock Jock (Scotsman)
(Usually abbreviated to 'sweaty', as in, 'Who wants to live in a country with a sweaty as Prime Minister?')

Sweeney Todd Flying Squad
(Sweeney Todd, the fictitious demon barber of Fleet Street who took delight in slitting his customers' throats with a razor, first appeared in print in 1846. Nearly a century later he came to be rhyming slang for the fast response unit of the Metropolitan Police, which, in the early 1920s had been christened the Flying Squad by an aptly named *Daily Mail* crime reporter, G. T. Crook. The rhyme earned wider recognition in 1975 with the hard-hitting ITV cops and robbers

series *The Sweeney*, which starred John Thaw as the maverick DI Jack Regan.)

Swiss army knife wife
(Perhaps because she has so many uses.)

Swiss banker wanker

Sylvester Stallone alone
(A modern alternative to Tod Sloan (see **Tod Sloan**) based on the sloth-faced star of the *Rocky* films.)

Syrup of fig wig
(A 1980s rhyme based on the dreaded laxative syrup of figs. The phrase is usually condensed to 'syrup', as in, 'The way Paul Daniels made his own syrup disappear to reveal a bald pate really was magic.')

T

Tale of Two Cities titties
(The title of Charles Dickens's 1859 novel, set in London and Paris, has produced rhyming slang as well as a popular spoonerism.)

Tapioca joker (cards)
(Bracketed with semolina in terms of a culinary experience, tapioca is a starchy grain that was used to make a poor man's rice pudding in post-war Britain.)

Tate and Lyle style
(From the company formed in 1921 by the merger of two rival sugar refiners – Henry Tate & Sons and Abram Lyle & Sons. Self-made millionaire Henry Tate (1819–99) had earlier used his fortune to found the Tate Gallery in London. He certainly had style.)

Taxicabs crabs (pubic lice)
(The natural successor to 'Hansom cabs' (see **Hansom cabs**), these 'taxis' are something that nobody wants to catch.)

Taxi rank bank

Tea and toast post
(A throwback to the time when the morning post in the UK used to arrive while you were having breakfast, as opposed to today's practice of any time after lunch – and then usually to the wrong house.)

Tea caddy Paddy (Irishman)

Tea leaf thief
(First heard around the start of the twentieth century and

still in all-too-frequent use, as in, 'Watch your wallet around here, there are a lot of tea leaves about.')

Tear and rip zip
(When zips were first introduced in the early twentieth century, there were widespread fears that they would catch, thereby tearing clothes. To allay public fears, a huge zip was put on show at the Wembley Empire Exhibition of 1924. By the end of the exhibition it had been zipped and unzipped three million times without catching.)

Teddy bear pear
(The term 'teddy bear' was first coined in 1906 by the US trade magazine *Playthings* and was named after President Theodore Roosevelt who, four years earlier, had made national headlines by refusing to shoot a bear cub while on a hunting trip in Mississippi.)

Teletubby hubby
(Based on the 1997–2001 children's TV series *Teletubbies*, created by Anne Wood, this rhyme clearly refers to a husband that is an overweight couch potato.)

Ten-ounce rump dump (shit)
(Almost certainly a movement to remember after eating such a large steak.)

Tennis racket jacket

Tent peg egg

Terry and Junes prunes
(After the cosy, undemanding suburban sitcom starring Terry Scott and June Whitfield that ran on BBC Television for eight very long years from 1979 to 1987.)

Terry Waite late
(The Archbishop of Canterbury's special envoy was kidnapped in 1987 in Beirut while trying to secure the release of hostages being held by Islamic militants. He was

not released until 1991, making him four years late for his flight home.)

Tex Ritter shitter (anus)
(After the US Western star (1905–74) whose real name wasn't Tex at all but the decidedly less cowboy-like Maurice.)

These and those toes

Theydon Bois noise
(Theydon Bois is an Essex village conveniently situated on the Central Line to make it an ideal venue for children on day trips from the East End of London in the 1950s. So its rural tranquillity was often replaced by a cauldron of noise.)

Thick and thin chin, grin

This and that cat

Thomas Edison medicine
(The prolific Thomas Edison (1847–1931) held over 1,093 US patents, his most famous invention being the electric light bulb.)

Thomas Tilling shilling
(Thomas Tilling (1825–93) founded a transport company in 1846 and by the time of his death had a stable of 4,000 horses pulling buses across London. The company went on to provide motorised buses throughout the UK until nationalisation in 1948.)

Thora Hird bird (young woman), turd
(An ironic rhyme since the formidable, Lancashire-born comedy actress (1911–2003) was scarcely anyone's idea of a 'bird' when the expression first caught on in the 1960s. And the association became even more surreal when she went on to present *Praise Be!* and advertise stairlifts.)

Three-card trick prick (penis)

Three-wheel trike dyke (lesbian)
(As in, 'Do you reckon she just likes dungarees or is she a three-wheeler?')

Threepenny bits tits, the shits (diarrhoea)
(Although originally introduced in the sixteenth century, the threepenny bit did not acquire its familiar 12-sided edge until the 1930s. The coin was phased out with the arrival of decimalisation in 1971.)

Thrust and throb knob
(A rhyme that does exactly what it says on the tin.)

Tia Maria diarrhoea
(From the Jamaican coffee liqueur introduced shortly after the Second World War.)

Tickle your fancy nancy (homosexual)

Tiddler's bait late
(Perhaps originating from the notion that a small boy fishing for tiddlers might be late home for his dinner.)

Tiddlywink drink
(The rhyme dates back to the mid-nineteenth century but the children's game did not adopt the name until much later, having been called Tiddledy-Winks on its invention in 1889. By the early twentieth century the rhyme had been shortened to 'tiddly', which has since become a familiar euphemism for 'slightly drunk', as in, 'Don't let Auntie Ethel have another sherry – she'll only get tiddly and start stripping off.')

Tijuana Brass arse
(You can't help thinking that ticket sales might have been slower to see 'Herb Alpert and his Arse'.)

Tilbury Docks socks
(A strategic fortress on the north bank of the Thames since the sixteenth century – Elizabeth I addressed her troops there prior to the anticipated arrival of the Spanish Armada

in 1588 – Tilbury acquired its docks in 1886 and has gone on to become London's principal port.)

Tin bath scarf
(Often shortened to 'tin', so that when venturing out into the cold you're advised to wear your 'tin and titfer' (see **Tit for tat**).)

Tin tack sack
(Dating back to the late nineteenth century, this has become the accepted rhyme for dismissal at work, as in, 'I see Bryan Robson's been given the tin tack again.')

Tin tank bank

Ting-a-ling ring
(As in, 'Look at the best man with his hand in his pocket playing with his ting-a-ling!')

Tit for tat hat
(The phrase 'tit for tat' meaning 'retaliation' is said to originate from the sixteenth century 'tip for tap' referring to an exchange of blows, although other sources claim it is based on the Dutch 'dit vor dat' meaning 'this for that'. Either way, it emerged as a rhyme for 'hat' in the late nineteenth century and was subsequently condensed to 'titfer' around 1930, in which form it enjoyed unparalleled success at a time when virtually everyone wore a hat. As the old saying went, 'If you want to get ahead, get a hat.')

Tit willow pillow
(What man could resist an invitation of 'Rest your head on my tits'?)

Toblerone alone
(Created by Theodor Tobler and Emil Baumann in Switzerland in 1908, the triangular bar of chocolate, nougat, almonds and honey has been a bestseller ever since.)

Toby jug mug (fool)
(First made by Staffordshire potters in the 1760s, a Toby jug

usually depicts a man in a long coat and tricorn hat holding a mug of beer. However the 'mug' in the rhyme refers to anyone daft enough to pay £100 at a car boot sale for a Toby jug that clearly has 'Made in Taiwan' stamped on the base.)

Tod Sloan alone
(Tod Sloan (1874–1933) was a highly successful American jockey who perfected a riding style known as the 'monkey crouch'. At the height of his fame he was surrounded by adoring women but he suffered an alarming fall from grace on both sides of the Atlantic amid allegations that he had been betting on his own races. His autobiography was prophetically titled *Tod Sloan by Himself* and he ended up dying alone. This cautionary tale of the fickleness of celebrity gave rise to the expression 'on your Tod Sloan', soon shortened to the more familiar 'on your tod'.)

Toilet roll dole
(So if a Cockney lends you a tenner because you're 'on the toilet', it's not to wipe your arse with.)

Tokyo Rose nose
(After the nickname given to Iva Toguri D'Aquino who tried to demoralise Allied troops by broadcasting Japanese propaganda over the airwaves during the Second World War.)

Tom and Dick sick
(The term 'Tom, Dick and Harry' meaning 'people in general' dates back to at least the nineteenth century but for the purposes of this rhyme the threesome became 'Harry, Tom and Dick'. From then on it was a familiar showbusiness tale. Harry decided he was better than the other two so he went solo, leaving Tom and Dick well...sick.)

Tom and Jerry merry
(From the cartoon cat and mouse created by William Hanna and Joseph Barbera for MGM in 1940, although Tom was anything but merry whenever Jerry clamped a mouse trap to the tip of his tail.)

Tom Cruise booze
(If the US actor were alcohol, he would of course be a short.)

Tom Dooleys goolies (testicles)
(The sad tale of Tom Dooley – a young American soldier executed in 1866 after being found guilty of murdering his sweetheart Laura Foster in North Carolina – has inspired several songs, including 1958 hits for the Kingston Trio and Lonnie Donegan. It has also produced one of the many rhymes for testicles, perhaps on the grounds that Tom himself was, in accordance with his trial verdict, damn well hung.)

Tom Hanks thanks
(Maybe the American actor signs cheques 'T Hanks'. Used as in, 'I spend all day running around after you and that's all the Tom Hanks I get.')

Tom Jones bones
(It's not every five minutes you hear the Welsh singer rhymed with 'bones' but it's not unusual.)

Tom Kite shite
(After the US Ryder Cup golfer.)

Tom Mix six
(Apart from Bambi and *The A Team*'s Mr T, US Western actor Tom Mix (1880–1940) must have been the fastest autograph writer in Hollywood.)

Tom Sawyer lawyer
(From the boy hero of four novels by US writer Mark Twain, beginning with *The Adventures of Tom Sawyer* (1876).)

Tom Thumb rum
(After the hero in English folklore who was no bigger than his father's thumb. So expect a very small measure of rum when ordering a 'Tom'.)

Tomato purée jury

Tomato sauce horse
(As in, 'You know that tomato I backed in the 2.30? It was so slow it had moss growing on it by the time it reached the finish.')

Tomcat doormat
(As in the potentially confusing, even cruel, 'Don't forget to wipe your feet on the tomcat before you step on my nice new carpet.')

Tomfoolery jewellery
(In use since the 1930s, chiefly as underworld slang for stolen jewellery. It was soon shortened to 'tom', as in, 'Did you really think I'd leave the tom in a biscuit tin? That's such a cliché.')

Tommy Dodd God
(Nobody knows whether the Tommy Dodd in this nineteenth-century rhyme ever existed, which is probably why it appealed to atheists.)

Tommy Farr bar
(A rhyme commemorating the Welsh-born former British heavyweight boxing champion (1914–86), nicknamed the 'Tonypandy Terror', who ran a pub in Sussex after retiring.)

Tommy guns the runs (diarrhoea)
(Inspired by the machine-gun fire with which a dose of diarrhoea splatters the toilet bowl.)

Tommy Steele jellied eel
(The traditional Cockney dish has the perfect partner in Bermondsey boy Tommy Steele, the one-time merchant seaman who was launched as Britain's answer to Elvis in 1956. When the hits dried up, he carved out a successful career in musicals.)

Tommy Trinder window
(With his pork-pie hat and catchphrase 'You lucky people',

fast-talking, London-born comedian Tommy Trinder (1909–89) was one of Britain's most popular entertainers from the 1930s onwards. In 1955 he became the first compere of ITV's *Sunday Night at the London Palladium* and later served as chairman of Fulham Football Club.)

Tommy Tucker sucker
(From the nursery rhyme – first published in 1829 – about orphan Little Tommy Tucker who sang for his supper.)

Tomtit shit
('Tomtit' is another name for a blue tit. In rhyming slang it dates from at least the 1940s and was the chosen lavatorial expression of Jim Royle in *The Royle Family*.)

Tony Blair hair

Tony Blairs flares
(Usually shortened to 'Tonys', this rhyme refers to flared trousers although in the latter years of his period in power, distress flares might have been more appropriate.)

Tony Slattery battery
(After the Cambridge-educated comedy actor who was rarely off the TV screen in the early 1990s.)

Tooting Bec peck (kiss)
(Based on the district of south London, as in, 'Go on, don't be shy – give her a Tooting on the cheek.')

Top hat prat
(Surely a comment by the working classes on the vacuous toffs who turn up at places like Royal Ascot in their top hats.)

Tord Grips nips (nipples)
(Swedish football coach Tord Grip was England assistant manager under Sven-Göran Eriksson. Grip's favourite musical instrument is the accordion, which he taught Sven (thereby prompting headlines about 'Sven's latest squeeze') but which can be hazardous to play for a big-breasted woman.)

Torquay United excited
(The last time anything exciting happened at the Devon football club was when the stadium roof blew off in 1930.)

Torvill and Dean queen (homosexual)
(In the 1980s Jayne Torvill and Christopher Dean were the golden partnership in ice skating – a sport that stereotypically appeals to confirmed bachelors.)

Touch me on the knob bob (shilling)
(A distinctly dodgy rhyme from the first half of the twentieth century, often abbreviated to 'touch me'. This may have given rise to the old joke, 'Can I touch you for [borrow] a shilling?' To which the reply was, 'Why not make it half a crown and go the whole way?')

Town crier liar

Trafalgar Square chair

Treacle tart sweetheart
(London market trader Pete Beale in *EastEnders* was prone to calling all the girls 'treacle'... except that because he couldn't roll his 'r's it came out as 'tweacle', which rather diminished the compliment.)

Treasure hunt cunt
(Perhaps because it is the anatomical equivalent of Aladdin's cave.)

Treble chance dance
(A rhyme taken from the name of a multiple bet on the football pools.)

Trick cyclist psychiatrist

Trolley and tram ham
(A rhyme celebrating two old forms of London public transport – the tram and the trolleybus. Trams originally faded out in the early 1950s and the last trolley bus ran in

the capital in 1962 although they kept going in Bradford for another ten years.)

Trombone phone
(This has continued to serve as a popular alternative to 'dog and bone' because of the link between the musical instrument and 'blower', which has been slang for 'telephone' since the 1920s.)

Trouble and strife wife
(First recorded in the early twentieth century, but although the term implies marital discord it is generally used affectionately. For example, it is doubtful whether Paul McCartney ever called Heather his 'trouble and strife'. The rhyme is sometimes reduced to 'trouble' so that 'trouble on the dog' means 'your wife is on the phone'.)

Troubles and cares stairs

Tumble down the sink drink
(A nineteenth-century rhyme later shortened to 'tumble-down' or even 'tumble'. But expect a slap in the face if you ask a girl on a first date if she fancies going for a tumble.)

Turkish bath laugh

Turkish Delight shite
(A confection of starch and sugar that originated in fifteenth-century Turkey, where it is known as *lokum*, meaning either 'mouthful' or 'contentment of the throat', depending on who you believe. Introduced to Britain in the nineteenth century, it has a soft, jelly-like texture and is often flavoured with rosewater, thereby giving it that distinctive pink colour. The rhyme acts as a warning against eating too much of the stuff.)

Turned and tossed lost

Turtle dove love

Turtle doves gloves
(First recorded in the 1850s and often abbreviated to 'turtles', as in the Cockney mother's cry, 'It's Cheltenham out, so don't forget to take your woolly turtles.')

Twist and twirl girl
(Sometimes condensed to 'twist' and perhaps inspired by the idea that girls can twist boys round their little fingers.)

Two and eight state (mess)
(Originating in the 1930s, this rhyme usually refers to a nervous state, as in, 'Since her old man ran off with that exotic dancer from Stepney, she's been in a proper two and eight.' But it can also apply to general untidiness, as in, 'Do something about your room – it's in a right two and eight.')

Two-bob bit shit
(After the two-shilling piece – or florin – that was in circulation in Britain from 1849 to 1971.)

Two thirty dirty

Parlez-vous Cockney?

I was having a game of horses and carts down the nuclear sub and all I needed was a rasher Tom Mix when some mackerel went and spilt his Richard Gere down me Callards.

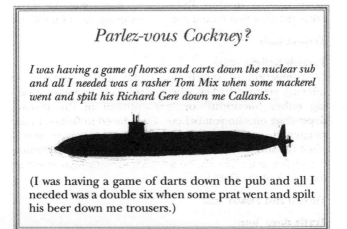

(I was having a game of darts down the pub and all I needed was a double six when some prat went and spilt his beer down me trousers.)

U

U2 flu
(After the Irish rock band, as in, 'Don't disturb her – she's in bed with U2.')

Ugly sister blister
(From the Ugly Sisters who gave Cinderella such a hard time. In Rossini's opera *La Cenerentola* – first performed in 1817 – they were called Clorinda and Thisbe but they have no set names and in modern pantomime are just as likely to be called Trinny and Susannah.)

Umbrella fella (boyfriend)

Uncle Ben ten
(Possibly derived from Uncle Ben's rice, first marketed in 1943.)

Uncle Bert shirt
(Usually shortened to 'uncle' – confusingly in view of the many other 'uncles' in Cockney rhyming slang – as in, 'What have you done with my clean uncle?')

Uncle Billy chilly

Uncle Bob knob (penis)

Uncle Dick prick (penis)

Uncle Fred bread

Uncle Gus bus
(If he is related to Uncle Bob or Uncle Dick, it might be wise to resist the temptation to hop on to Uncle Gus.)

Uncle Mac quack (doctor)
('Uncle Mac' was the broadcasting name of Derek McCulloch

(1897–1967) who joined BBC radio in 1926 as an announcer and in the 1930s presented *Children's Hour*, closing each edition with his comforting sign-off line, 'Goodnight, children everywhere.' He went on to voice Larry the Lamb in *Toytown* and from 1954 to 1965 presented the radio request show *Children's Favourites*, in which he vainly tried to steer his young listeners away from pop music in favour of Bach or 'Nellie the Elephant'. The rhyme may originate from the fact that just as a 'quack' isn't a real doctor, so Uncle Mac wasn't your real uncle.)

Uncle Ned bed
(First recorded in the 1920s, this rhyme, too, can be shortened to 'uncle', as in, 'Come on, time to get out of uncle!')

Uncle Reg veg
(Hence that Cockney favourite, 'Hands and feet and two Uncle Reg.')

Uncle Sam lamb

Uncle Ted bed
(He obviously shares with Uncle Ned.)

Uncle Wilf the filth (police)

Uncle Willy silly

Uncles and aunts plants
(As in, 'I'm just going up the allotment to water me uncles and aunts.')

Union Jack back
(Mentioning the flag of the United Kingdom often indicates a painful back, as in, 'I'm having real trouble with me Union just lately.')

Up and down brown (ale)

Up and under thunder
(A Rugby League term much loved by colourful BBC

commentator Eddie Waring (1910–86) but used here in the sense of people getting up and hiding under the stairs during a night-time storm.)

Up the aisle doggy style (sexual position)
(As in, 'The only reason you're marrying her is because she takes it up the aisle.')

Uri Geller Stella (Artois)
(After the Israeli/British psychic unique for bending spoons and for choosing Michael Jackson as his best man when renewing his wedding vows in 2001.)

V

Valentine Dyalls piles
(From the British actor (1908–85) known as 'The Man in Black' for his eerie narration of the long-running BBC radio horror series *Appointment With Fear* (1943–55).)

Vancouver hoover
(Based on the city in British Columbia, Canada, as in, 'Can't you even be bothered to lift your plates while I vancouver around you?'

Vanity Fair chair
(From the 1848 novel of that title by William Makepeace Thackeray (1811–63).)

Vauxhall Cavalier queer (homosexual)
(This entry can be dated by the lifespan of the car (1976–94). The model was probably only selected for its rhyming capacity but the image of Cavaliers from the English Civil War – all feathers and moustaches – also suggests a degree of effeminacy and probably explains why Charles I lost to the altogether more butch Roundheads.)

Vauxhall Novas Jehovah's (Witnesses)
(Another from the British motor manufacturer, this time the Nova, which was produced between 1983 and 1993. One country where the car didn't do too well was Spain, perhaps understandably since '*no va*' means 'won't go'. The rhyme may stem from the fact that it was just as easy – although less satisfying – to shut the door on a Vauxhall Nova as on a Jehovah's Witness.)

Vera Lynn gin
(The 'Forces' Sweetheart' of the Second World War has

become so associated with gin that it is frequently shortened to 'Vera'.)

Victoria Beckham Peckham
(Hard to imagine the stylish Posh Spice shopping in the land of Del Boy. There probably isn't even a decent Gucci store up Rye Lane. (See also **Posh and Becks**.))

Vincent Price ice
(After the US actor (1911–93), famous for his chilling roles in horror movies.)

Vincent van Gogh cough
(The Dutch painter (1853–90) was beset by depression, hallucinations and paranoia that he was being poisoned. In his later years he committed himself to a mental asylum and sliced off part of his left ear. So a cough was the least of his problems.)

Von Trapp crap
(The Austrian von Trapp family were a group of singers whose escape from the Nazis inspired *The Sound of Music*, earning them the eternal gratitude of Julie Andrews and the Salzburg Tourist Board.)

Parlez-vous Cockney?

I was just enjoying a discreet Sherman in the Ilie Nastase when some Willy Wonka starts banging on the George Bernard screaming that he's desperate for a Donald Trump.

(I was just enjoying a discreet wank in the khazi when some plonker starts banging on the door screaming that he's desperate for a dump.)

W

Wallace & Gromit vomit
(The plasticine man and dog residents of 62 West Wallaby Street were created by Nick Park and made their debut in Aardman Animations' *A Grand Day Out* in 1990. The pair have won three Oscars – more than the likes of John Gielgud, Bette Davis and Sean Connery – meaning that Gromit can lord it over Lassie as Top Dog in Hollywood. The rhyme could be linked to Wallace's excessive intake of Wensleydale cheese.)

Wallace Beery query
(After the US actor (1885–1949) who played Long John Silver in the 1934 film of *Treasure Island*.)

Walnut Whip kip
(For the uninitiated a Walnut Whip is a chocolate cone with a whipped vanilla fondant filling and a walnut on top. Launched in 1910, it is Nestlé Rowntree's oldest current brand and it is estimated that one walnut whip is eaten every two seconds in the UK.)

Walter Mitty kitty
(Based on the fictional character in James Thurber's story *The Secret Life of Walter Mitty*, first published in 1939. Mitty was a meek, mild man but also a vivid fantasist and the term 'Walter Mitty character' has subsequently been applied to anyone who roughly fits that description. In rhyming slang it is often shortened to 'Walter', as in, 'How much bread is left in the Walter?')

Wanstead Flats spats
(A late nineteenth-century rhyme from the days when spats – short fabric covers that were worn on the lower leg to

protect the wearer's shoes from mud – were the height of fashion. They were rhymed with an open space in Essex, which once formed the southern end of Epping Forest.)

Watch and chain brain
(Wristwatches for men did not become popular until the First World War, a watch and chain being the order of the day prior to that. This rhyme related to intelligence – or lack of it – leading to remarks such as, 'You'll have to excuse him, his watch is a bit slow.')

Water bottle throttle

Watford Gap slap
(After the geographical break in the hills in Northamptonshire. Used as in, 'If he carries on like that he's going to get a Watford Gap.')

Wayne Rooney loony
(A fitting rhyme for the young footballer who paid to have sex with a gap-toothed Liverpool grandmother affectionately known as the 'Auld Slapper', an episode which has at least spared him being taunted with the chant from opposing fans of 'You couldn't score in a brothel.')

Weasel and stoat coat
(This familiar rhyme may stem from the fact that both animals are renowned for their fine coats. In the TV series *Minder*, Arthur Daley objected to having his collar felt in case the police crumpled his smart camel-hair 'weasel'.)

Weaver's chair prayer

Wee Georgie Wood good
(Commemorating the 4ft 9in British music-hall comedian (1894–1979) who spent much of his career playing children – an early Jimmy Krankie.)

Weeping willow pillow

West End thespian lesbian

West Ham Reserves nerves
(After the East End football club and usually shortened to 'West Hams', as in, 'You're really starting to get on my West Hams.')

Westminster Abbey cabbie, shabby
(The rhyme with 'shabby' is clearly ironic as there are few smarter buildings in London than Westminster Abbey.)

Whip and top strop
(From the child's toy of the nineteenth and early twentieth centuries. The rhyme is often shortened to 'whip', as in, 'Your love and kisses is in a bit of a whip today.')

Whisky and soda Skoda
(Based on the premise that a whisky and soda goes faster than a Skoda.)

Whistle and flute suit
(Dating back to the early twentieth century, this rhyme has become so established that it has even crossed the Atlantic where it has been adopted by a New York fashion collection. It is usually shortened to 'whistle', as in, 'I've only gone and spilt rocking horse down me new whistle!')

Whistle and toot loot

White Cliffs of Dover over
('Over' and 'Dover' have been a rhyming couple since Vera Lynn's stirring rendition of 'There'll Be Bluebirds Over The White Cliffs of Dover'. The 1941 song – written by Americans Walter Kent and Nat Burton while British and German planes were fighting it out above Kent – looked forward to a time when the war would be over and peace would reign once more in the skies above the famous White Cliffs. The fact that there never has been – and probably never will be – a bluebird over the White Cliffs of Dover (because the bird is native to the composers' homeland) was apparently considered only a minor flaw in the lyrics. Obviously 'blackbird' didn't have the same ring to it.)

White mice ice
(As in the unlikely request, 'Do you want white mice in your Scotch?')

Whitechapel apple
(From the area of east London where Jack the Ripper went on a murderous spree in 1888. However, the rhyme is more likely to be the product of the district's long-standing association with Spitalfields fruit and vegetable market until it moved to a new location in 1991.)

Wicked rumours bloomers (knickers)

Widow Twankey hanky (handkerchief)
(After the name of the comic washerwoman – normally played by a man – in the pantomime *Aladdin*. She has almost certainly washed a lot of handkerchiefs in her time.)

Wilbur Wright flight
(The American Wright brothers Wilbur (1867–1912) and Orville (1871–1948) were the pioneers of aviation who, in 1903, made the first powered flight in an aeroplane. Some 80 years later Orville lent his name to ventriloquist Keith Harris's green duck who famously couldn't fly but wished he could.)

Wild West vest

Wilfrid Brambell gamble
(Irish actor (1912–85) whose role as Shepherd's Bush rag and bone man Albert Steptoe in the classic TV sitcom *Steptoe and Son* masked a difficult private life involving alcoholism and homosexuality. Constantly referred to in the show as 'you dirty old man', Brambell was in fact a dapper dresser who detested the famous scene where his character ate pickled onions in the bath because he smelt of them for the rest of the week.)

Will o' the wisps crisps

William Hague vague
(The former Conservative leader was entitled to be vague

after claiming that he used to drink fourteen pints of beer a day. Mind you, having a photo of Margaret Thatcher above your bed – as the teenage Hague did – would turn anyone to drink.)

William Joyce voice
(Alias 'Lord Haw Haw', William Joyce (1906–46) possessed the most hated voice in the Second World War as he broadcast Nazi propaganda over British airwaves. He was executed for treason.)

William Tell smell
(Based on the fourteenth-century Swiss folk hero who led the Austrians a merry dance and whose exploits with a crossbow and apple inspired the ITV game show *The Golden Shot* (1967–75), thus bringing the world Anne Aston and Bernie the Bolt.)

Wills Whiff syph (syphilis)
(Wills Whiffs were a brand of small cigars popular in the 1950s and made by British cigarette manufacturers W. D. & H. O. Wills.)

Willy Wonka plonker
(After the enchanting character in Roald Dahl's children's book *Charlie and the Chocolate Factory* and played by Johnny Depp in the 2005 film.)

Wilson Pickett ticket
(A rhyme taken from the name of the US soul singer (1941–2006).)

Wind and kite web site

Winnie the Pooh shoe
(Created by English author A. A. Milne (1882–1956), the lovable bear with a taste for honey first appeared in book form in 1926.)

Winona Ryder cider
(The wealthy US actress mysteriously went shoplifting for

clothes in a Beverly Hills store in 2001. Perhaps she was under the influence of strong cider.)

Witches' cackle wedding tackle (penis)

Wooden pews news

Wooden plank Yank
(A term that implies a certain lack of intelligence among American tourists in London.)

Woolly woofter poofter

Woolwich and Greenwich spinach
(From two districts of south-east London where the second is pronounced 'Grinidge'.)

Working classes glasses

Worms and snails fingernails
(Often shortened to 'worms', as in, 'I'm just going to trim me worms.')

Worzel Gummidge rummage
(The talking scarecrow in books by British writer Barbara Euphan Todd (1890–1976) made his debut in print in 1936. In the 1979 TV series, Worzel was played by former Doctor Who Jon Pertwee.)

Wyatt Earp burp
(After the Wild West marshal (1848–1929) who kept law and order in Dodge City and participated in the infamous Gunfight at the OK Corral in 1881.)

Are you a real fridge freezer?

1. What would you be wearing if you had an Irish jig?

2. If somebody poured you a Vera, what would you be drinking?

3. In rhyming slang, what is your hard labour?

4. Which fictional detective means 'fake'?

5. If you were Darren Day, what might you be?

6. If you complimented a lady on her Mary Ellens, to what would you be referring?

7. How much money is a Rio?

8. Why might you wear a bottle of cola on your head?

9. Where might you find Ilie Nastase?

10. Why would you wear your Simon Schamas for Uncle Ted?

Answers: 1. Wig 2. Gin (Vera Lynn) 3. Neighbour 4. Sexton Blake 5. Gay 6. Her big breasts (melons) 7. A grand (Rio Ferdinand) 8. It's a bowler (hat) 9. The khazi (toilet) 10. They're your pyjamas for bed

XYZ

X Files piles
(A 1990s rhyme taken from the title of the cult US mystery series in which FBI agents Fox Mulder (David Duchovny) and Dana Scully (Gillian Anderson) investigated cases of the paranormal.)

Parlez-vous Cockney?

I was feeling a bit Sue Lawley so I went down the Uncle Mac to see if he could give me something to stop me being Tom and Dick in the black and white. He stuck his bell ringers so far down my nanny I thought I was going to Wallace & Gromit all over him.

(I was feeling a bit poorly so I went down the 'quack' to see if he could give me something to stop me being sick in the night. He stuck his fingers so far down my throat I thought I was going to vomit all over him.)

Yankee Doodles noodles
(See **Macaroni**)

Yarmouth bloater motor
(From the Norfolk fishing port of Great Yarmouth, renowned for its smoked fish, a UK bloater being a smoked herring. This is not to be confused with a North American bloater which is a different fish altogether.)

Yellow silk milk

Yorkshire Tyke mike (microphone)
('Tyke' is slang for a Yorkshireman.)

You and me tea
(Dating back to the nineteenth century and suggesting tea for two.)

You must crust
(A simple rhyme from post-war Britain urging children to eat the crusts off their bread.)

Yours and ours flowers

Zachary Scotts the trots (diarrhoea)
(From the Texan actor (1914–65) who specialised in playing scoundrels. The rhyme is often shortened to 'Zacharys', as in, 'I'm just off to the Kermit cos I've got a touch of the Zacharys.')

Zane Grey pay (wages)
(Zane Grey (1875–1939) was a US writer of adventure stories and surprisingly gets the nod for the pay rhyme over home-grown talent such as Lady Jane Grey, broadcaster Robin Day and Queen guitarist Brian May.)

Zig and Zag shag
(After the puppet aliens from the planet Zog who appeared on Channel 4's *The Big Breakfast* in the 1990s.)

Zippy and Bungle jungle
(Zippy, a creature of indeterminate breed, and Bungle the bear were characters from the long-running ITV children's series *Rainbow*. (See also **George and Zippy**.))

Zorba the Greek take a leak (urinate)
(Based on the title of the 1946 novel by Nikos Kazantzakis which became a box-office hit in 1964 starring Anthony Quinn, who was not Greek at all but Irish/Mexican. The film in turn spawned the instrumental hit 'Zorba's Dance' by Marcello Minerbi, who was Italian.)

Zulu Dawn horn (erection)
(From the title of the 1979 film that marked the centenary of the Zulu uprising. The link between first thing in the morning – 'dawn' – and an erection requires no further elaboration.)

Parlez-vous Cockney?

I don't want your skin and blister coming to our Otis – she's a right Billy Bragg and she'll end up copping off with the pie and liquor.

(I don't want your sister coming to our wedding – she's a right slag and she'll end up copping off with the vicar.)

ENGLISH – RHYMING SLANG

A

Ace (playing cards) Ricky Gervais

Actor Max Factor

Advice lump of ice

AIDS ace of spades, shovels and spades

Ale Daily Mail

All dayer (drinking session) Gary Player

All nighter jet fighter

All right shiny and bright

Alone (On your own) Darby and Joan, Sylvester Stallone, Tod Sloan, Jack Jones, Toblerone

Anus (Arsehole, Ring, Shitter) Samantha Janus, Elephant & Castle, Roy Castle, South Pole, Pearly King, banana fritter, council gritter, Gary Glitter, Spam fritter, Tex Ritter

Appendix Jimi Hendrix

Apple Sistine Chapel, Whitechapel

Arm Chalk Farm, false alarm, lucky charm

Army daft and barmy, Kate Carney

Arris (see **Arse**)

Arse (Arris, Ass, Bum, Jacksie) blade of grass, bottle and glass, Häagen-Dazs, Khyber Pass, Tijuana Brass, Rolf Harris, Myleene Klass, big bass drum, bottle of rum, bubble gum, date and plum, kingdom come, Queen Mum, London taxi

Arsehole (see **Anus**)

Ass (see **Arse**)

Aunt garden plant

B

BO Riddick Bowe

Bacardi Laurel and Hardy

Back Cadbury's Snack, Cilla Black, Penny Black, Roof rack, Union Jack

Bad Jack the Lad, sorry and sad

Bad breath Megadeth

Bail Royal Mail

Baked beans kings and queens

Baker Long Acre

Balls (testicles) (Bollocks, Goolies, Knackers) Berlin Walls, Cobbler's awls, Davina McCalls, Henry Halls, marble halls, market stalls, Max Walls, Niagara Falls, orchestra stalls, Castor and Pollux, fun and frolics, Jackson Pollocks, Tom Dooleys, cream crackers, Jacob's Crackers, Michael Schumachers, nutcrackers

Balti Basil Fawlty

Banana Gertie Gitana

Banger (sausage) Bernhard Langer

Bank Armitage Shank, cab rank, fish and tank, iron tank, rattle and clank, taxi rank, tin tank

Banned Jimmy Shand

Bar Jack tar, Jean Michel Jarre, Tommy Farr

Barber Dover harbour

Barmy Dad's Army, Monty's army, Salvation Army

Barrow cock sparrow

Basin Charlie Mason, Fortnum & Mason

Bath hat and scarf

Battery charm and flattery, Tony Slattery

Batty Carlo Gatti

Beak (see **Magistrate**)

Beard just as I feared, strange and weird

Beaver (see **Vagina**)

Bed Uncle Ned, Uncle Ted

Beef itchy teeth

Beer (Bitter, Bottle of Bass, Brown (ale), Guinness, Lager, Light (ale), Mild, Stella (Artois), Stout) Christmas cheer, Germaine Greer, pig's ear, Richard Gere, apple fritter, Gary Glitter, kitty litter, laugh and titter, beggar boy's ass, up and down, photo finish, Forsyte Saga, day and night, stage fright, Marty Wilde, David Mellor, Nelson Mandela, Paul Weller, Uri Geller, salmon and trout

Beers Britney Spears, Ray Mears

Beg Doctor Legg

Beggar Ewan McGregor

Beginner Lilley and Skinner

Belch Raquel Welch

Believe Adam and Eve

Bell hair gel, Little Nell

Belly Auntie Nelly, Darby Kelly, George Melly, New Delhi

Bender (see **Gay**)

Bent (homosexual) (see **Gay**)

Berk Charlie Smirke

Best Mae West

Bet deep in debt

Beverage Edna Everage

Bevy (drink) Don Revie

Big Porky Pig

Big 'un (see **Penis**)

Bigot Lester Piggott

Bike Dick Van Dyke, Iron Mike

Bill Muswell Hill

Bingo George and Ringo

Bird (girl) lemon curd, Richard the Third, Thora Hird

Bird cage Jimmy Page

Bitch Miss Fitch

Bitchy Nicole Richie

Bitter (see **Beer**)

Black coalman's sack

Blade (knife) First aid

Blind Golden Hind

Blister Ugly sister

Bloke heap of coke

Blonde On Golden Pond

Bloomers (see **Knickers**)

Blotto (see **Drunk**)

Blow job (Gam, Go down, Oral sex) corn on the cob, plate of ham, Divine Brown, Ant 'n' Decs

Blower (see **Phone**)

Boat frog in the throat, hat and coat

Bob (see **Shilling**)

Body Big Ears and Noddy

Bog (toilet) (Crapper, Khazi, Throne) Boss Hogg, Captain's log, Kermit the frog, Frank Zappa, Ilie Nastase, rag and bone

Bogey Jimmy Logie, old fogey

Boil (spot) Bodie and Doyle, Conan Doyle

Bollocks (see **Balls**)

Bones sticks and stones, Tom Jones

Bonkers marbles and conkers

Book Captain Hook, fish hook, Rookery Nook

Bookie cream cookie

Boots Burdett Coutts, daisy roots, King Canutes

Booze pick and choose, River Ouse, Tom Cruise

Boozer (see **Pub**)

Bored Cyril Lord

Borrow Sodom and Gomorrah

Boss dead loss, Edmundo Ros

Bottle Aristotle, Gerry Cottle

Bottle of Bass (see **Beer**)

Bounce (a cheque) half-ounce

Bouncer (doorman) half-ouncer

Bounty (bar) Stockport County

Bow and arrow sparrow

Bowels Simon Cowells

Bowler (hat) bottle of cola

Bowling J. K. Rowling

Box (theatre) Charles James Fox

Boy pride and joy, Rob Roy

Boy Scout brussel sprout

Bra ooh la la, Roseanne Barr

Braces airs and graces, Ascot Races

Brain down the drain, watch and chain

Brakes Charlie Drakes

Brandy fine and dandy, Mahatma Gandhi

Brat Jack Sprat

Bread needle and thread, Uncle Fred

Breasts (Jugs, Knockers, Melons, Tits, Titties) cabman's rests, Georgie Bests, carpets and rugs, Mods and Rockers, Mary Ellens, Ballroom Blitz, fainting fits, first-aid kits, moonlight flits, oven mitts, threepenny bits, Bristol Cities, Tale of Two Cities

Breath life and death

Brick Dublin trick

Bride fat and wide, mother's pride

Brogues (shoes) Kylie Minogues

Broke (penniless) coals and coke, heart of oak

Brolly (see **Umbrella**)

Broom bride and groom

Brother manhole cover

Brown (ale) (see **Beer**)

Brown (halfpenny) Camden Town

Brown (snooker ball) half a crown

Brush Ian Rush

Buffoon Geoff Hoon

Bullet Ruud Gullit

Bum (see **Arse**)

Bummer Joe Strummer, John Selwyn Gummer

Bunion pickled onion

Burp Wyatt Earp

Bus don't make a fuss, swear and cuss, Uncle Gus

Bus timetable Aesop's fable

Butter mutter and stutter, stammer and stutter

Button Len Hutton

Parlez-vous Cockney?

I'd like to order a portion of Yankee Doodles, some Duchess of York with rats and mice, sweet and sour Goldie Hawns and fried itchy teeth.

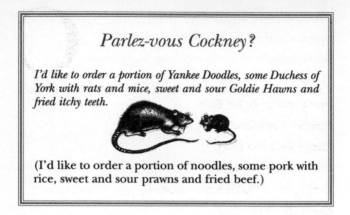

(I'd like to order a portion of noodles, some pork with rice, sweet and sour prawns and fried beef.)

C

Cab (Taxi) Andy McNab, flounder and dab, Sherbet Dab, smash and grab, Joe Baksi

Cabbie Westminster Abbey

Cadge coat and badge

Café Colonel Gaddafi

Cake give and take, Sexton Blake

Can (safe) Peter Pan

Cancel Nigel Mansell

Candle saucepan handle

Cans (headphones) Desperate Dans

Cap game of nap

Car (Motor) jamjar, haddock and bloater, Yarmouth bloater

Cards (playing) Coldstream Guards

Cardy (cardigan) Linda Lusardi

Carrots Polly parrots

Cash (Readies) Arthur Ashe, bangers and mash, pie and mash, sausage and mash, Nelson Eddys

Cat cooking fat, this and that

Catch ya later Kat Slater

Ceiling funny feeling

Cell (prison) flowery dell

Central heating Ronan Keating

Chair here and there, lion's lair, Lionel Blair, Trafalgar Square, Vanity Fair

Chairs Owen Nares

Chalk Duke of York, Lambeth Walk

Chancer ballet dancer

Change (money) rifle range

Chapel pineapple

Charlie (see **Cocaine**)

Charmer Jeffrey Dahmer

Chassis Shirley Bassey

Chat chew the fat, Frank and Pat

Cheap Meryl Streep

Cheating Angus Deayton

Cheek (nerve) hide and seek

Cheeky cockaleekie

Cheese balmy breeze, John Cleese, stand at ease

Cheque chicken's neck, Duchess of Teck, goose's neck, Gregory Peck, Jeff Beck, nervous wreck, pain in the neck

Chest bird's nest, east and west, Mae West

Chief corned beef

Child molester (Nonce) Charlie Chester, bacon bonce

Chill Jimmy Hill

Chilly Uncle Billy

Chin Andy McGinn, Errol Flynn, Gilbey's gin, thick and thin

Chink (Chinese) rink-a-dink

Chip lucky dip

Chips Jagger's lips, jockeys' whips

Choice Rolls-Royce

Choker Bram Stoker

Chum Fruit Gum

Chunder (see **Vomit**)

Church left in the lurch, seek and search

Cider runner and rider, Shaun Ryder, Winona Ryder

Cigar La-di-da, Spanish guitar

Cigarette lighter kung fu fighter

Clanger coat hanger

Clap (see **Gonorrhoea**)

Claret (blood) boiled beef and carrot

Cleaner semolina

Clink (see **Jail**)

Clock dickory dock

Closed doublet and hosed

Clothes line grape vine

Clown Charlie Brown

Clue Danny La Rue, didgeridoo, pot of glue, Scooby-Doo

Clutch Starsky and Hutch

Coach cockroach

Coal merry old soul

Coat all afloat, bucket afloat, Dover boat, nanny goat, pound note, Quaker Oat, weasel and stoat

Cocaine (Charlie, Line, Powder) Kurt Cobain, Bob Marley, Boutros Boutros-Ghali, Gianluca Vialli, oats and barley, Patsy Cline, Niki Lauda

Cock (see **Penis**)

Cockney David Hockney

Cockney rhyming slang Chitty Chitty Bang Bang

Cod Richard Todd

Coffee Everton toffee, sticky toffee

Cold Cheltenham Gold, Naughton and Gold, potatoes in the mould, soldier bold

Collar Oxford scholar, shout and holler

Collar and tie swallow and sigh

Comb garden gnome, Millennium Dome

Con Elton John

Concertina constant screamer

Conk (see **Nose**)

Cook babbling brook

Cop (police officer) (Copper, Filth) lemon drop, pork chop, bottle and stopper, clodhopper, grasshopper, Uncle Wilf

Copper (see **Cop**)

Cords (corduroy trousers) House of Lords

Corner Johnny Horner

Corns Cape Horns

Couch kangaroo pouch

Cough Darren Gough, horse and trough, on and off, Vincent van Gogh

Cousin baker's dozen

Cow Chairman Mao

Coward Frankie Howerd

Crabs (pubic lice) Beattie and Babs, Hansom cabs, marble slabs, taxicabs

Cramp rising damp

Crap (see **Shit**)

Crapper (see **Bog**)

Crash sausage and mash

Creeps Samuel Pepys

Crime lemon and lime

Cripple raspberry ripple

Crisps will o' the wisps

Crook babbling brook

Crotch (groin) Lord Sutch, rabbit hutch, Starsky and Hutch

Crust you must

Cum (see **Semen**)

Cunt (see **Vagina**)

Cup dog and pup

Cup of tea Jack Dee

Cupboard Mother Hubbard

Curry Ruby Murray

Curtains Richard Burtons

D

Daft fore and aft

Dance Jack Palance, kick and prance, treble chance

Danger Stewart Granger

Dark Jurassic Park

Darts horses and carts

Daughter bottle of water, bricks and mortar, soap and water

Dead brown bread, Father Ted, gone to bed, loaf of bread

Deaf Mutt and Jeff

Deal jellied eel

Denial River Nile

Dense garden fence

Devil Gary Neville

Diarrhoea (Runs, Shites, Shits, Trots) Tia Maria, Radio Ones, Tommy guns, Arabian Nights, banana splits, three-penny bits, red hots, Zachary Scotts

Dice cats and mice

Diesel pop goes the weasel

Diet Brixton riot, peace and quiet

Digs (lodgings) Ronnie Biggs

Dinner Michael Winner, saint and sinner

Dirty hundred to thirty, two thirty

Doddle Glenn Hoddle

Dog London fog

Doggy style (sexual position) up the aisle

Dogs (greyhound racing) cherry hogs

Dole (Giro) Adrian Mole, jam roll, Nat King Cole, Old King Cole, rock 'n' roll, sausage roll, toilet roll, Night Boat to Cairo

Dollar Oxford scholar

Doner (kebab) Sinead O'Connor

Door Andrea Corr, George Bernard Shaw, Roger Moore, Rory O'Moore

Doormat tomcat

Dope (cannabis) (Draw, Hash, Weed) Bob Hope, Jack Straw, Jack Flash, Oliver Reed

Dosh (see **Money**)

Doss Hugo Boss

Double (in darts) rasher and bubble

Dough (see **Money**)

Dozen country cousin

Drain Spanish Main

Draught George Raft

Draw (see **Dope**)

Drawers (see **Knickers**)

Dreams custard creams

Dress more or less, mustard and cress

Drill Benny Hill

Drink Engelbert Humperdinck, kitchen sink, Lily the Pink, tiddlywink, tumble down the sink

Dripping (fat) Doctor Crippen

Drugs kisses and hugs, Persian rugs

Drunk (Blotto, Pissed, Plastered, Slaughtered, Smashed, Tiddly) elephant's trunk, Mickey Monk, Santa's Grotto, booed and hissed, Brahms and Liszt, fog and mist, Gorillas in the Mist, hand and fist, Oliver Twist, Schindler's List, Scotch mist, lord and mastered, son and daughtered, pebble-dashed, Bo Diddley, Newton and Ridley

Dump (see **Shit**)

Dwarf Canary Wharf

Dyke (see **Lesbian**)

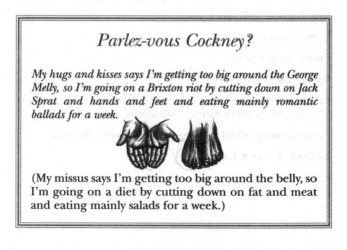

Parlez-vous Cockney?

My hugs and kisses says I'm getting too big around the George Melly, so I'm going on a Brixton riot by cutting down on Jack Sprat and hands and feet and eating mainly romantic ballads for a week.

(My missus says I'm getting too big around the belly, so I'm going on a diet by cutting down on fat and meat and eating mainly salads for a week.)

E

Eager Christian Ziege

Ear bottle of beer, glass of beer

Early Liz Hurley, Pepsi and Shirlie

Earner Anthea Turner

Earner, nice little Bunsen burner

Ears King Lears, lords and peers, sighs and tears, Southend Piers

Easy ham and cheesy, lemon squeezy

Egg borrow and beg, tent peg

Eight garden gate

Email Alexei Sayle

Epsom races airs and graces

Erection (Horn) general election, early morn, Mountains of Mourne, September Morn, Zulu Dawn

Evens (betting odds) Major Stevens, Shakin' Stevens

Excited Torquay United

Eyes mince pies

F

Face Boat Race, Chevy Chase, fillet of plaice, Hale and Pace, kipper and plaice, Peyton Place

Facts brass tacks

Fag (cigarette) (Smoke, Woods (Woodbines)) Harry Wragg, jet lag, oily rag, puff and drag, laugh and joke, do me goods

Fags (cigarettes) Oxford bags

Fair enough hairy muff

Fairy Julian Clary

Fake Sexton Blake

Fanny (see **Vagina**)

Fare grey mare

Farmers (see **Haemorrhoids**)

Fart apple tart, Billy Smart, broken heart, D'Oyly Carte, false start, horse and cart, Lionel Bart, raspberry tart

Fat Jack Sprat

Father soap and lather

Favour cheesy Quaver

Feel orange peel

Feet dog's meat, plates of meat

Fella (boyfriend) umbrella

Fever Robinson and Cleaver

Fiancée darling Beyoncé

Fib spare rib

Fiddle hey diddle diddle

Fight left and right, read and write

Filth (see **Cop**)

Fine (penalty) bottle of wine, Calvin Klein

Fingernail slug and snail

Fingernails worms and snails

Fingers bell ringers

Fire Anna Maria, Black Maria

First (degree result) Geoff Hurst, Pattie Hearst, raging thirst

Fish Lillian Gish

Five man alive

Fiver deep sea diver, Lady Godiva, Minnie Driver, scuba diver

Fix Hans Blix

Flares (trousers) Dan Dares, Lionel Blairs, Rupert Bears, Tony Blairs

Flicks (cinema) Stevie Nicks

Flies Morecambe and Wise

Flight Wilbur Wright

Floor Mrs Moore, Rory O'Moore

Flowers April showers, early hours, yours and ours

Flu inky blue, U2

Flutter (bet) grumble and mutter

Flying Squad Sweeney Todd

Fob (watch) kettle and hob

Food in the mood

Fool garden tool

Foot chimney and soot

Football pools April Fools

Foreman Joe O'Gorman

Foreskin lose or win

Fork Duke of York, roast pork

Four knock at the door

Freak Ancient Greek

Freezer Bacardi Breezer

French, the bloody muddy trench

Frenchies park benches

Fridge London Bridge, Stamford Bridge

Friend Mile End

Frig (see **Masturbates)**

Fright Ian Wright

Front (nerve) James Hunt

Frown Gordon Brown

Fuck (see **Sex)**

Fucker chicken plucker

Funnel Blackwall Tunnel

Parlez-vous Cockney?

Did you hear about the left and right down the rub-a-dub last night? One sweaty got hit over the crust with a Peter O'Toole and the other one ended up with cut apple pips, boiled beef and carrot all down his dicky, a kick in the Tom Dooleys and a real Morris Minor.

(Did you hear about the fight down the pub last night? One Scotsman got hit over the head with a stool and the other one ended up with cut lips, blood all down his shirt, a kick in the goolies and a real shiner.)

G

Gal (see **Girl**)

Gam (see **Blow job**)

Gamble Wilfrid Brambell

Garage horse and carriage, Steve Claridge

Garden Dolly Varden

Gargle Arthur Scargill

Gay (Bender, Bent, Homo, Iron, Nancy, Poof, Poofter, Queen, Queer, Shirtlifter) C&A, Darren Day, Doris Day, fromage frais, home and away, Howards' Way, Milky Way, Leo Fender, bottle of scent, Clark Kent, Duke of Kent, Stoke-on-Trent, Perry Como, Lenny the Lion, tickle your fancy, collar and cuff, iron hoof, woolly woofter, Nellie Dean, pork and bean, Torvill and Dean, Brighton Pier, chandelier, ginger beer, King Lear, Vauxhall Cavalier, Mr Shifter

Geezer fridge freezer, Julius Caesar, lemon squeezer

Ghost pillar and post

Giggles Squadron Leader Biggles

Gin Brian O'Linn, needle and pin, Nell Gwynn, Vera Lynn

Gin and tonic philharmonic

Girl (Gal) ivory pearl, mother of pearl, ribbon and curl, twist and twirl, Pall Mall

Giro (see **Dole**)

Git strawberry split

Glasses (Specs) mountain passes, working classes, Gregory Pecks

Gloves turtle doves

Go Scapa Flow

Go down (see **Blow job**)

God Tommy Dodd

Goggle box (see **Telly**)

Golf caddie Puff Daddy

Gonorrhoea (Clap) ogle and leer, pony and trap

Good Robin Hood, Wee Georgie Wood

Goolies (see **Balls**)

Gout in and out, salmon and trout

Grand (£1,000) bag of sand, Rio Ferdinand

Grass old iron and brass

Grass (police informant) (Nark) duck's arse, car park, grass in the park, Noah's Ark

Gravel Jimmy Savile

Gravy Army and Navy

Greek bubble and squeak

Greens (vegetables) has beens, Nellie Deans

Grey night and day

Grief Omar Sharif

Grin thick and thin

Ground safe and sound

Growler (see **Vagina**)

Grumble rhubarb crumble

Guinness (see **Beer**)

Gut (stomach) Limehouse Cut

Guts fruit and nuts, Newington Butts

Gutter bread and butter

Gym Fatboy Slim

H

Haddock Bessie Braddock, Fanny Cradock

Haemorrhoids (Farmers, Piles) Clement Freuds, Emma Freuds, Judith Chalmers, Adrian Chiles, Belinda Carlisles, Chalfont St Giles, Farmer Giles, Jeremy Kyles, Michael Miles, Nobby Stiles, Nuremberg Trials, Plymouth Argyles, Rockford Files, Seven Dials, Valentine Dyalls, X Files

Hair Barnet Fair, Biffo the Bear, Fred Astaire, Tony Blair, Alf Garnett (barnet)

Hair, pubic (Minge, Pubes) Fanny Blair, Edinburgh Fringe, Rubik's Cubes

Hairy Sharleen Spiteri

Half (pint of beer) cow and calf

Ham trolley and tram

Hammer stutter and stammer

Hand brass band, German band

Handle Harry Randall

Hands Margate sands

Handsome Marilyn Manson

Handy Jack and Dandy

Hanky (handkerchief) Widow Twankey

Hard bread and lard, Marquis de Sade

Harsh Jodie Marsh

Hash (see **Dope**)

Hat (Tile) ball and bat, tit for tat, penny-a-mile

Head ball of lead, crust of bread, Judge Dredd, loaf of bread, lump of lead, ruby red

Head (of family) daily bread

Heart jam tart, stop and start, strawberry tart

Heaven S Club 7

Hell ding dong bell

Hemp Martin Kemp

Hill Jack and Jill

Hole drum roll

Home gates of Rome

Homo (see **Gay**)

Honda Henry Fonda

Honours Jimmy Connors

Hooker (see **Whore**)

Hooter (see **Nose**)

Hoover Vancouver

Horn (see **Erection**)

Horse bottle of sauce, tomato sauce

Hot Alan Knott, peas in the pot

House cat and mouse, Mickey Mouse

Hubby Teletubby

Huff cream puff

Hump (anger) petrol pump

Hymen Bill Wyman

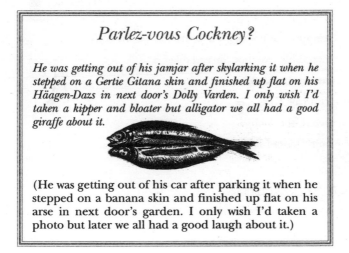

Parlez-vous Cockney?

He was getting out of his jamjar after skylarking it when he stepped on a Gertie Gitana skin and finished up flat on his Häagen-Dazs in next door's Dolly Varden. I only wish I'd taken a kipper and bloater but alligator we all had a good giraffe about it.

(He was getting out of his car after parking it when he stepped on a banana skin and finished up flat on his arse in next door's garden. I only wish I'd taken a photo but later we all had a good laugh about it.)

I

Ice sugar and spice, Vincent Price, white mice

Incredible Anchor Spreadable

Insane David Blaine

Iron (see **Gay**)

Itch Little Tich

Itchy Lionel Richie

J

Jacket Desmond Hackett, fag packet, tennis racket

Jacksie (see **Arse**)

Jail (Clink, Nick, Slammer) bucket and pail, ginger ale, Jimmy Nail, moan and wail, rusty nail, kitchen sink, shovel and pick, Franz Klammer

Jam Amsterdam, baby's pram

Jap (Japanese) rat trap

Jeans baked beans, Bethnal Greens, Dixie Deans, Harpers and Queens, Milton Keynes, Steve McQueens

Jehovah's (Witnesses) Vauxhall Novas

Jellied eel Tommy Steele

Jelly Mother Kelly

Jew (Yid) four by two, Cisco Kid, slippery Sid

Jewellery tomfoolery

Jive duck and dive

Job corn on the cob, couple of bob, dog's knob, knocker and knob

Jock (Scotsman) sweaty sock

Johnny (condom) Reggie and Ronnie

Joke can of Coke, Diet Coke, egg yolk

Joker (playing cards) tapioca

Judge Barnaby Rudge, chocolate fudge, inky smudge, smear and smudge

Jugs (see **Breasts**)

Jumper Kuala Lumpur

Jungle Zippy and Bungle

Jury tomato purée

Parlez-vous Cockney?

That John's a lucky fillet. He fluked the half a crown by getting a hit and miss off the rinky dink, somehow potted the bald head and then put the Marti Pellow into a different Davy Crockett to the one he was aiming for.

(That John's a lucky sod. He fluked the brown by getting a kiss off the pink, somehow potted the red and then put the yellow into a different pocket to the one he was aiming for.)

K

Karaoke hokey cokey

Keen James Dean

Kettle Hansel and Gretel, stinging nettle

Key Bruce Lee

Keys Cheddar cheese, dancing fleas, honey bees, knobbly knees

Khazi (see **Bog**)

Kid (child) dustbin lid, God forbid, saucepan lid

King (playing cards) Highland fling

Kinky Natasha Kaplinsky

Kip (sleep) jockey's whip, lucky dip, Sherbet Dip, Walnut Whip

Kipper Jack the Ripper

Kiss heavenly bliss, hit and miss

Kitty Walter Mitty

Knackered cream crackered, Kerry Packered

Knackers (see **Balls**)

Knees biscuits and cheese, Cecil Gees, chips and peas

Knickers (Bloomers, Drawers) Alan Whickers, Bill Stickers, wicked rumours, Diana Dors

Knife drum and fife, man and wife

Knob (see **Penis**)

Knockers (see **Breasts**)

Kraut (German) lager lout

L

Laces dirty faces

Ladder Blackadder

Ladies' (toilet) Rosie O'Grady's

Lager (see **Beer**)

Lamb Uncle Sam

Lark Joan of Arc, Noah's Ark

Late Catherine Tate, Cow & Gate, Harry Tate, Terry Waite, tiddler's bait

Later alligator, Christian Slater

Lather (state) how's your father?

Laugh giraffe, Steffi Graf, Turkish bath

Lawyer Tom Sawyer

Lazy Gert and Daisy

Leak (see **Piss**)

Legs (Pins) bacon and eggs, clothes pegs, cribbage pegs, Mystic Megs, pin pegs, Scotch eggs, Scotch pegs, Rin Tin Tins

Leicester Square Euan Blair

Lesbian (Dyke) West End thespian, Magnus Pyke, mountain bike, Raleigh bike, three- wheel trike

Liar Bob Cryer, deep fat fryer, Dunlop tyre, town crier

Lie cherry pie, collar and tie

Lies pork pies

Light (ale) (see **Beer**)

Line (see **Cocaine**)

Lips apple pips, PG Tips

Lisp Quentin Crisp

Liver bow and quiver, cheerful giver, Swanee River

Loan shark Cutty Sark

Lodger Artful Dodger, Jolly Roger

Look butcher's hook, Captain Cook

Loon Keith Moon

Loony Wayne Rooney

Loose Mother Goose

Loot whistle and toot

Lorry sad and sorry

Lost turned and tossed

Love turtle dove

Lunch Brady Bunch, kidney punch

Parlez-vous Cockney?

I was sent down the lollipop to buy Uncle Reg for Michael Winner, but the polly parrots were Dot Cotton, the Spanish waiters were coalman's and the Woolwich and Greenwich wasn't worth the bread.

(I was sent down the shop to buy veg for dinner, but the carrots were rotten, the potatoes were black and the spinach wasn't worth the money.)

M

Mad Mum and Dad

Magistrate (Beak) garden gate, bubble and squeak

Marge (margarine) little and large

Married cash and carried

Mason David Jason, Larry Grayson

Masturbates (Frig, Toss, Wank) Gareth Gates, live gig, Jonathan Ross, Kate Moss, polish and gloss, Barclays Bank, J. Arthur Rank, Jodrell Bank, Sherman tank

Match down the hatch

Matches cuts and scratches

Mate china plate, dinner plate

Meal Ian Beale

Meat hands and feet

Medicine Thomas Edison

Melons (see Breasts)

Memory Dick Emery

Menace Les Dennis

Menstrual cycle George Michael

Mental chicken oriental, Radio Rental

Merry Tom and Jerry

Mess Eliot Ness, Rudolf Hess

Mike (microphone) Yorkshire Tyke

Mild (see Beer)

Milk Acker Bilk, lady in silk, satin and silk, yellow silk

Mind bacon rind

Mine host (publican) dripping toast

Minge (see Hair, pubic)

Minger Jerry Springer

Minute cock linnet

Missus (see Wife)

Moaner Kerry Katona

Moans Bridget Jones

Mobi (mobile phone) Obi-Wan Kenobi

Money (Dosh, Dough, Wad, Wedge) bees and honey, bread and honey, Bugs Bunny, Easter bunny, orange squash, Rogan Josh, Russell Crowe, Ken Dodd, Percy Sledge

Monte Carlo Gary Barlow

Moody Punch and Judy, Richard and Judy

Moon silver spoon

Morning gypsy's warning

Motor (see Car)

Moustache dot and dash

Mouth north and south

Muddle kiss and cuddle

Mug (drinking) barge and tug

Mug (fool) steam tug, stone jug, Toby jug

Mum finger and thumb

Murder iron girder

Muscles greens and brussels

Mutton Billy Button

N

Nag paper bag

Nail monkey's tail

Nancy (see **Gay**)

Nappy Cheeky Chappie

Nark (police informant) (see **Grass**)

Neck bushel and peck, Gregory Peck

Needle Jeremy Beadle

Neighbour hard labour

Nerves West Ham Reserves

Nervous Peter Purves

News bottle of booze, wooden pews

Newspaper linen draper

Nice sugar and spice

Nick (see **Jail**)

Night black and white

Nightie God almighty

Nine Brighton line

Nipper (child) fly tipper

Nipple (Nips) raspberry ripple, Tord Grips

Nippy (cold) George and Zippy

Nips (see **Nipple**)

Noise box of toys, girls and boys, Theydon Bois

Nonce (see **Child Molester**)

Noodles Yankee Doodles

Nose (Conk, Hooter) Axl Rose, doublet and hose, fireman's hose, I suppose, Tokyo Rose, glass of plonk, pea shooter

Number Samantha Mumba

Nun hot cross bun

Nutter brandy butter, bread and butter, peanut butter

Nutty chip butty

Parlez-vous Cockney?

My dream afternoon is lying on the Gordon, plates up with a Germaine in me German band and watching the down the hatch on the KY jelly.

(My dream afternoon is lying on the sofa, feet up with a beer in me hand and watching the match on the telly.)

O

Oats John O'Groats

Off Frank Bough

Off his rocker Jarvis Cocker

Oil ruin and spoil

Old silver and gold

Old Bailey Arthur Daley

Old lady Slim Shady

Old man (husband or father) frying pan, pot and pan

On the cheap Sooty and Sweep

On the labour (exchange) beggar my neighbour

On the pull John Bull

On your own (see **Alone**)

One buttered bun

Onions corns and bunions

Oral sex (see **Blow job**)

Organ (musical) Captain Morgan

Orgasm fit and spasm

Out of order Allan Border

Over White Cliffs of Dover

Own goal Ashley Cole

P

Paddy (Irishman) goodie and baddie, tea caddy

Pain Frasier Crane, Hanger Lane, Michael Caine, Shania Twain

Pair Sonny and Cher

Pakistani Reg Varney

Pan Isle of Man

Pants Adam Ants, fleas and ants, Pirates of Penzance

Paper skyscraper

Pardon Osama bin Laden

Park Noah's Ark

Park (a vehicle) skylark

Parole jam roll

Parrot Jasper Carrott

Party hale and hearty, Moriarty, Russell Harty

Pathetic Charlton Athletic

Pay (wages) Zanc Grey

Pear teddy bear

Peck (kiss) Tooting Bec

Pecker (see **Penis**)

Peckham Victoria Beckham

Pee (see **Piss**)

Pen Dirty Den

Penalty fare Cherie Blair

Penis (Big 'un, Cock, Knob, Pecker, Prick, Tadger, Todger, Wedding tackle) Mars and Venus, Barry McGuigan, almond rock, Blackpool rock, grandfather clock, thrust and throb, Uncle Bob, Black & Decker, Boris Becker, dipstick, Hampton Wick, Lionel Hampton, pogo stick, three-card trick, Uncle Dick, fox and badger, Artful Dodger, witches' cackle

Penny Abergavenny, Jack Benny

Pension stand to attention

Pepper dirty leper

Pest string vest

Phone (Blower) Darby and Joan, dog and bone, eau de Cologne, jelly bone, Sharon Stone, trombone, Percy Thrower

Photo kipper and bloater

Piano Joanna

Pick (tool) Paddy and Mick

Pickle slap and tickle

Pickles Harvey Nichols

Pictures (cinema) Dolly mixtures

Piddle (see **Piss**)

Pie Captain Bligh, smack in the eye

Piles (see **Haemorrhoids**)

Pill Damon Hill, Pebble Mill

Pill, contraceptive Fanny Hill, Harry Hill, Jack and Jill

Pillow tit willow, weeping willow

Pinch (steal) half-inch

Pink (snooker ball) rinky dink

Pins (see **Legs**)

Pipe artichoke ripe, cherry ripe

Piss (Leak, Pee, Piddle, Slash, Tinkle) Arthur Bliss, cuddle and kiss, gypsy's kiss, hit and miss, snake's hiss, Zorba the Greek, Christopher Lee, Peters and Lee, Jimmy riddle, Nelson Riddle, pig in the middle, bangers and mash, J. Carrol Naish, Johnny Cash, Leslie Ash, Ogden Nash, Pat Cash, pie and mash, Rip Van Winkle

Pissed (see **Drunk**)

Pisshole savoury rissole

Pitch hedge and ditch

Pizza Mona Lisa

Plan Jackie Chan, Manfred Mann

Plants uncles and aunts

Plastered (see **Drunk**)

Plate Alexander the Great, Harry Tate, Pearly Gate

Play (theatrical) Evelyn Laye

Please hairy knees

Plonker Willy Wonka

Plug little brown jug

Pocket chain and locket, Davy Crockett, Lucy Locket, penny locket, sky rocket

Poker jolly joker

Pole (nationality) sausage roll

Ponce (pimp) Alphonse, Charlie Ronce

Pong (see **Smell**)

Pony (£25) macaroni

Poof (see **Gay**)

Poofter (see **Gay**)

Poor on the floor

Poorly Sue Lawley

Pope bar of soap

Pork Duchess of York

Porn Frankie Vaughan, Johnny Vaughan

Port (wine) didn't ought

Poser bulldozer, Carl Rosa

Post (mail) beans on toast, Holy Ghost, Sunday roast, tea and toast

Potato (Spuds) Spanish waiter, Roy Hudds

Pound Huckleberry Hound, lost and found, merry-go-round

Powder (see **Cocaine**)

Pox (Syph, VD) boots and socks, cardboard box, Dairy Box, East India Docks, Goldilocks, Jack in the box, Surrey Docks, bang and biff, lover's tiff, Wills Whiff, bumble bee

Prat mackerel and sprat, paper hat, top hat

Prawn Goldie Hawn

Prayer chocolate éclair, weaver's chair

Preggers (pregnant) (Up the duff) Keith Cheggers, Peter Brough

Price Anneka Rice, Condoleezza Rice, nits and lice, snow and ice

Prick (see **Penis**)

Priest bag of yeast, dirty beast

Printer Alan Minter

Prison warder Harry Lauder

Prunes Terry and Junes

Psychiatrist trick cyclist

Pub (Boozer) nuclear sub, rub-a-dub, battle cruiser

Pubes (see **Hair, pubic**)

Puff Nellie Duff

Pull (chat up) cotton wool

Punter Billy Bunter, Hillman Hunter

Purse doctor and nurse

Pyjamas panoramas, Simon Schamas

Parlez-vous Cockney?

I reckon my Edmundo Ros is Darren Day. At Captain Kirk yesterday he wore a pink Peckham, yellow almonds, suede St Louis, spent a lot of Harry Lime rabbiting to the new Rob Roy and they ended up going for a tiddlywink together.

(I reckon my boss is gay. At work yesterday he wore a pink tie, yellow socks, suede shoes, spent a lot of time talking to the new boy and they ended up going for a drink together.)

Q

Quack (doctor) Uncle Mac

Quarter (of hashish) Janet Street-Porter

Queen (Elizabeth II) baked bean, runner bean

Queen (homosexual) (see **Gay**)

Queer (homosexual) (see **Gay**)

Query Wallace Beery

Quid (£1) bin lid

R

Rabbits monks' habits

Rain Andy Cain, pleasure and pain

Randy port and brandy

Rave Comedy Dave

Raver cheesy Quaver

Razor Frankie Fraser, House of Fraser

Readies (see **Cash**)

Red (snooker ball) bald head

Rent Burton-on-Trent, Duke of Kent

Rice rats and mice

Ride Charlie Pride

Right harbour light, Isle of Wight

Ring (jewellery) Highland fling, ting-a-ling

Ring (rectum) (see **Anus**)

Rip acid trip

River shake and shiver

Road frog and toad

Roger (see **Sex**)

Rolls (Royce) Camilla Parker Bowles

Room bride and groom

Rotten Dot Cotton

Rough Brian Clough, Mickey Duff

Round (of drinks) hare and hound

Row (argument) bull and cow, pantomime cow

Rum finger and thumb, Tom Thumb

Rummage Worzel Gummidge

Runs (see **Diarrhoea**)

Parlez-vous Cockney?

He always claimed his soap and lather was a famous Max Factor but it turns out he was telling porkies – the frying pan had nothing more exciting than a couple of bob as a bloody Gay Gordon.

(He always claimed his father was a famous actor but it turns out he was telling lies – the old man had nothing more exciting than a job as a bloody traffic warden.)

S

Sack Big Mac, last card of the pack, Roberta Flack, tin tack

Sad Alan Ladd

Salad romantic ballad

Saloon bar balloon car

Salt Earls Court, squad halt

Sandals Roman candles

Sandwich maker Kula Shaker

Sarnie (sandwich) Giorgio Armani

Sauce Air Force, rocking horse

Saucer Geoffrey Chaucer

Sausage rolls Beyoncé Knowles

Saveloy Myrna Loy

Saw bear's paw, Denis Law, mother-in-law

Say so cocoa

Scar Mars bar

Scarf centre-half, half and half, tin bath

Scary Bloody Mary, Mariah Carey

Score Ali MacGraw, Jude Law

Score (£20) Bobby Moore

Scotch (see **Whisky**)

Scouser Mickey Mouser

Screw (see **Sex**)

Sea housemaid's knee

Semen (Cum, Spunk) Bob Beamon, Pedigree Chum, rattle and hum, Maria Monk, pineapple chunk

Sense pounds and pence, shillings and pence

Sex (Fuck, Roger, Screw, Shag) Oedipus Rex, Posh and Becks, crispy duck, Donald Duck, Friar Tuck, Konnie Huq, lame duck, rubber duck, jammie dodger, Barney McGrew, Melvyn Bragg, Zig and Zag

Shabby Westminster Abbey

Shades (sunglasses) Jack of Spades

Shag (see **Sex**)

Shakes, the Hattie Jacques

Shambles Jackie Brambles

Shandy Andy Pandy, Beano and Dandy

Shares Rupert Bears

Shave Chas and Dave, Mexican wave, ocean wave, rant and rave

Shilling (Bob) rogue and villain, Thomas Tilling, doorknob, touch me on the knob

Shiner (black eye) Morris Minor, ocean liner

Ship halfpenny dip

Shirker office worker

Shirt dicky dirt, Uncle Bert

Shirtlifter (see **Gay**)

Shit (Crap, Dump, Shite) bottomless pit, brace and bit, Brad Pitt, Eartha Kitt, hard hit, tomtit, two-bob bit, Andy Capp, pony and trap, Von Trapp, camel's hump, Donald Trump, Forrest Gump, ten-ounce rump, Barry White, fly a kite, Tom Kite, Turkish Delight

Shite (see **Shit**)

Shites (see **Diarrhoea**)

Shits (see **Diarrhoea**)

Shitter (see **Anus**)

Shitty Elgin City

Shocker Costantino Rocca

Shoe Winnie the Pooh

Shoes five to twos, Jimmy Choos, Looby Loos, ones and twos, rhythm and blues, St Louis blues

Shooter (gun) Phil the Fluter

Shop Cheggers Plays Pop, lollipop, Mrs Mopp

Short (drink) magistrate's court

Shoulders Noddy Holders, rocks and boulders

Shout brussel sprout

Shovel Lord Lovell

Shower Blackpool Tower, David Gower, Eiffel Tower

Showers Austin Powers

Shrimp Colonel Blimp

Shut Jabba the Hutt

Sick Moby Dick, spotted dick, Tom and Dick

Sikh oil leak

Silly daffadown dilly, Piccadilly, Uncle Willy

Singer mangle and wringer

Single Mandy Dingle

Sister skin and blister

Six pick up sticks, Tom Mix

Sixty-six clickety click

Skint After Eight mint, Bernie Flint, boracic lint, Murray mint, Polo mint

Skiver backseat driver

Skoda whisky and soda

Sky shepherd's pie

Slag Billy Bragg

Slammer (see **Jail**)

Slap brandy snap, Watford Gap

Slash (urinate) (see **Piss**)

Slaughtered (see **Drunk**)

Sleep Bo Peep

Slightly Keira Knightley

Slippers big dippers, Jack the Rippers, pair of kippers

Smart lemon tart

Smashed (see **Drunk**)

Smell (Pong, Stink, Whiff) heaven and hell, William Tell, Anna May Wong, Hong Kong, Suzie Wong, pen and ink, Jimmy Cliff

Smitten Atomic Kitten

Smoke cough and choke

Smoke (cigarette) (see **Fag**)

Smoke (London) old oak

Snake George Blake

Sneeze bread and cheese

Snore lion's roar

Snout (see **Tobacco**)

Snow buck and doe

Snuff blindman's buff

Soap Band of Hope, Bob Hope, Cape of Good Hope

Socks almond rocks, diamond rocks, Tilbury Docks

Sod fillet of cod

Sofa Gordon the Gopher

Son bath bun, currant bun

Song ding dong

Soon Alfie Moon

Sores Dudley Moores

Soup bowl the hoop, loop the loop

Spanner Elsie Tanner

Sparrow bow and arrow

Spats Wanstead Flats

Speak bubble and squeak

Specs (see **Glasses**)

Speech Southend beach

Speed (amphetamines) Lou Reed

Spick (Spaniard) oil slick

Spider sit beside her

Spinach Woolwich and Greenwich

Splinter Harold Pinter

Spoon blue moon, Lorna Doone, man on the moon

Spot jelly tot, Randolph Scott, Selina Scott

Spouse boiler house, Dangermouse

Spuds (see **Potato**)

Spunk (see **Semen**)

Squatter pig's trotter

Squeal (inform on) conger eel

Squirrel nice one, Cyril

Stab doner kebab

Stain Cynthia Payne, Michael Caine

Stairs apples and pears, dancing bears, troubles and cares

Starbucks Lisa Tarbucks

Starvin' Hank Marvin

State (mess) Harry Tate, two and eight

Station poor relation

Stays (corset) Bryant and Mays

Steak Joe Blake

Steak and kidney Kate and Sidney

Stella (Artois) (see **Beer**)

Stench Dame Judi Dench

Step Johnny Depp

Stew Battle of Waterloo

Still (photo) Beecham's Pill

Stilton (cheese) Paris Hilton

Stink (see **Smell**)

Stocking reeling and rocking, simply shocking

Stockings Silas Hockings

Stolen goods Little Red Riding Hoods

Stool Peter O'Toole

Stop thief hot beef

Story Frankie Dettori, Jackanory

Stout (see **Beer**)

Straight six and eight

Stranger Glasgow Ranger, Queens Park Ranger

Streak Dawson's Creek

Street ain't it a treat, field of wheat

Stretch Jack Ketch

Strides (see **Trousers**)

Stripper herring and kipper

Strop whip and top

Stunner air gunner

Style Tate and Lyle

Sub (pay advance) rub-a-dub

Sucker Tommy Tucker

Suit bowl of fruit, whistle and flute

Sulk Incredible Hulk

Sun bath bun, currant bun

Sun (newspaper) currant bun

Suntan lotion Billy Ocean

Suspenders no surrenders

Swear Lord Mayor, rip and tear

Sweetheart treacle tart

Syph (syphilis) (see **Pox**)

T

Table Betty Grable, Cain and Abel

Tadger (see **Penis**)

Taff (Welshman) riff raff

Tail alderman's nail

Tail (prostitute) (see **Whore**)

Tailor Sinbad the Sailor

Takeaway Jay Kay

Tale Binnie Hale, Daily Mail, Newgate Gaol

Talk Duke of York, rabbit and pork

Talker Johnnie Walker, Murray Walker

Tan Charlie Chan, Steely Dan

Tanner (sixpence) lord of the manor

Tart horse and cart, kick start

Tax Ajax, bees' wax

Taxi (see **Cab**)

Tea Rosie Lee, you and me

Tears Britney Spears

Teeth Edward Heath, Hampstead Heath, roast beef

Telly (Goggle box) custard and jelly, KY jelly, Marie Corelli
Roger Mellie, Nervo and Knox

Ten Big Ben, Bill and Ben, cock and hen, Uncle Ben

Tenner Ayrton Senna, Jim Fenner, Paul McKenna

Tennis Les Dennis

Thanks Tom Hanks

Thick (stupid) king dick, Paddy and Mick, Queen Vic

Thief leg of beef, tea leaf

Thieves Jimmy Greaves

Thin needle and pin

Third (degree result) Douglas Hurd

Thirst Geoff Hurst

Thirty Burlington Bertie

Thirty-four dirty whore

Throat nanny goat

Throne (see **Bog**)

Throttle water bottle

Thrush (female genital complaint) Basil Brush

Thumb Jamaica rum

Thunder Stevie Wonder, up and under

Ticket bat and wicket, Wilson Pickett

Ticket inspector Hannibal Lecter

Tiddly (see **Drunk**)

Tie Peckham Rye

Tights fly-by-nights, Snow Whites

Tile (see **Hat**)

Till Benny Hill

Time Harry Lime, lager and lime

Time (prison sentence) birdlime

Times (newspaper) nursery rhymes

Tinkle (see **Piss**)

Tired barb-wired

Tits (see **Breasts**)

Titties (see **Breasts**)

Toast Holy Ghost, Mickie Most

Toaster roller coaster

Tobacco (Snout) Oi Jimmy Knacker, salmon and trout

Todger (see **Penis**)

Toes buttons and bows, Sebastian Coes, these and those

Tomatoes Stars and Garters

Tongue Jimmy Young

Tools April Fools, Crown Jewels

Toss (see **Masturbates**)

Tosser dental flosser

Tote canal boat

Totty Bruno N'Gotty

Towel Enoch Powell, mortar and trowel, Sandy Powell

Toy girl and boy

Traffic warden Gay Gordon

Train hail and rain, John Wayne, struggle and strain

Trainers (shoes) Claire Rayners, Gloria Gaynors

Tram baa lamb, bread and jam

Tramp halfpenny stamp, hurricane lamp, paraffin lamp

Travel Jimmy Savile

Trots (see **Diarrhoea**)

Trouble Barney Rubble

Trousers (Strides) Callard & Bowsers, council houses, round the houses, Herbie Hides, Jekyll and Hydes

Trowel Baden-Powell, bark and growl

True Irish stew

Truth Maud and Ruth

Tube (London Underground) Oxo cube

Tune stewed prune

Tunnel Sally Gunnell

Turd Douglas Hurd, lemon curd, Richard the Third, Thora Hird

Turk Captain Kirk

Turkey Pinky and Perky

Twat (see **Vagina**)

Twenty Horn of Plenty

Twenty-four Pompey whore

Twig (understand) earwig

Twins needles and pins

2:1 (degree result) Attila the Hun

2:2 (degree result) Desmond (Tutu)

Tyre Billy Liar

Parlez-vous Cockney?

OK, cheese grater, that's a philharmonic, a Bill Oddie, two Uri Gellers, a Major Loder, a pimple with Vincent, a cow and calf of laugh and titter – cos I'm driving – a Tom Thumb and blackcurrant and three packets of Cleese and bunion will o' the wisps.

(OK, waiter, that's a gin and tonic, a vodka, two Stellas, a whisky and soda, a Scotch with ice, a half of bitter – cos I'm driving – a rum and blackcurrant and three packets of cheese and onion crisps.)

U

Umbrella (Brolly) Auntie Ella, Stan and Ollie

Undertaker overcoat maker

Undies (underpants) Eddie Grundies

Up the duff (see **Preggers**)

V

VD (veneral disease) (see **Pox**)

Vagina (Beaver, Cunt, Fanny, Growler, Twat) Elizabeth Regina, Morris Minor, Sigourney Weaver, Bargain Hunt, Berkshire Hunt, eyes front, Gareth Hunt, growl and grunt, grumble and grunt, James Blunt, National Front, treasure hunt, Jack and Danny, nook and cranny, Orphan Annie, Arthur Fowler, bowler hat, honey pot

Vague William Hague

Van Peter Pan

Veg Uncle Reg

Very best John West

Vest east and west, Wild West

Vicar half a nicker, pie and liquor

Viewing (house) J. R. Ewing

Villain Bob Dylan, Harold Macmillan

Vin blanc (white wine) plinkety plonk

Virus Billy Ray Cyrus

Voddie (vodka) Bill Oddie

Voice Hobson's choice, William Joyce

Vomit (Chunder) Wallace & Gromit, Stevie Wonder

Parlez-vous Cockney?

I've been Elton Johnned – that lemon squeezer's taken me for a right Toby jug, writing a goose's that has half ounced all the way to the cab rank.

(I've been conned – that geezer's taken me for a right mug, writing a cheque that has bounced all the way to the bank.)

W

Wad (see **Money**)

Wager John Major

Wages greengages, rock of ages

Waistcoat Charlie Prescott

Waiter cheese grater, hot potato

Wales Canterbury Tales

Walk ball of chalk, Duke of York

Wander Jane Fonda

Wank (see **Masturbates**)

Wanker merchant banker, monkey spanker, oil tanker, Ravi Shankar, Sri Lanka, Swiss banker

Warm Somerset Maugham

Watch bottle of Scotch

Water didn't oughta, fisherman's daughter

Weather hat and feather

Web site wind and kite

Wedding Otis Redding

Wedding tackle (see **Penis**)

Wedge (see **Money**)

Weed (see **Dope**)

Week in Malaga Noel Gallagher

Weight Alfred the Great, pieces of eight

West (End of London) jacket and vest

Wheels (transport) jellied eels

Whiff (see **Smell**)

Whiskers hammer and discus

Whisky (Scotch) gay and frisky, gold watch, pimple and blotch

Whisky and soda Major Loder

Whistle Partick Thistle

Whore (Hooker, Tail) boat and oar, Jane Shore, six to four, one-time looker, brass nail

Whore house flea and louse

Wife (Missus) bread knife, carving knife, drum and fife, Duchess of Fife, Sporting Life, Swiss army knife, trouble and strife, hugs and kisses, love and kisses

Wig guinea pig, Irish jig, syrup of fig

Win nose and chin

Wind Jenny Lind

Window burnt cinder, Tommy Trinder

Windscreen wipers Billie Pipers

Windy Mork and Mindy

Wine Calvin Klein, River Tyne

Winkles Granny's wrinkles

Winner chicken dinner, hot dinner

Wishes pots and dishes

Woman gooseberry puddin'

Woods (Woodbines) (see **Fag**)

Word dicky bird

Work Captain Kirk, Kathy Burke, smile and smirk

Wrong Pete Tong

Parlez-vous Cockney?

I'm dreading making a Southend beach at my bricks and mortar's Otis. I think I'll need a few Engelberts down my Gregory to calm my West Ham Reserves or I'll get a sorry and sad dose of the Zacharies.

(I'm dreading making a speech at my daughter's wedding. I think I'll need a few drinks down my neck to calm my nerves or I'll get a bad dose of the trots.)

XYZ

Yank (American) board and plank, septic tank, wooden plank

Yanks (Americans) ham shanks

Years donkey's ears

Yellow (snooker ball) Marti Pellow

Yen Bill and Ben

Yes Brown Bess

Yid (see **Jew**)

Yuppie Hush Puppy

Zip tear and rip

Parlez-vous Cockney?

I once went to airs and graces and put a bag of sand on a tomato sauce at Shakin' Stevens but the deep in debt was Andy Capp in the handicap and left me so coals and coke I had to Duke of York to the gates of Rome.

(I once went to Epsom races and put a grand on a horse at evens but the bet was crap in the handicap and left me so broke I had to walk home.)